New Every Morning

NANCY ROTH

New Every Morning

Meditating on Hymns for Year C

 Church Publishing Incorporated, New York

Library of Congress Cataloging-in-Publication Data

Roth, Nancy, 1936–
    New Every Morning: meditating on hymns for year C /
    Nancy Roth.
        p.   cm.
    Includes bibliographical references.
    ISBN 0-89869-336-5 (pbk.)
    1. Hymns—Devotional use. 2. Church year meditations.
3. Episcopal Church—Hymns—History and criticism. 4. Hymns, English—United States—History and criticism. I. Title.

BV340 .R69 2000
264'.23—dc21   00-059047

Church Publishing Incorporated
445 Fifth Avenue
New York NY 10016

http://www.churchpublishing.org

5 4 3 2 1

Acknowledgments

I could not have managed this project without the helpful editorial advice and moral support of my husband Bob. I also owe a debt of gratitude to Mary Louise VanDyke, the custodian of the Dictionary of American Hymnology at the Oberlin College Library. Her enthusiasm for this project and her contributions to my research have been invaluable.

In memory of my father

Robert Foster Moore

1902–1964

Contents

Introduction

New Every Morning: Meditating on Hymns for Year C is the third volume in my series of books providing background material and meditations based on selected hymns in *The Hymnal 1982*. There were many possible ways to organize these books: chronologically, according to the dates of the texts; theologically, according to the themes of the hymns; or even numerically, beginning with Hymn 1, "Father, we praise thee, now the night is over," and ending in a blaze of glory with Hymn 720, the National Anthem. However, the publisher and I finally chose to organize them according to the pattern of the church year, beginning in Advent and including all Sundays and major Holy Days. This arrangement encourages meditation on those hymns that reflect the themes of each liturgical season, and also provides a practical format for those who wish to use hymnody in preaching and teaching. I selected hymns from the lists suggested for Years

A, B, and C by Marion J. Hatchett in *Hymnal Studies Five: A Liturgical Index to the Hymnal 1982.*

It probably goes without saying that you do not need to follow the sequence of the church year in reading these books. You can dip into this volume, as well as into the other two—*A Closer Walk* (Year A) and *Awake, My Soul!* (Year B)—at random, using the index in the back of each one. At the end of this volume, you will find an index for the entire series. You will probably want to have a copy of *The Hymnal 1982* or *Poems of Grace: Texts of The Hymnal 1982* close at hand, although I am told that many of the meditations can stand on their own.

Since I began this project, I have discovered with each passing year what a wealth of spirituality and inspiration is contained in our hymn tradition. As I travel around the country leading workshops based on my work, I find that meditating on hymn texts is a way to integrate head and heart. I have become increasingly aware that the hymnody of the church is a rich—and often overlooked—resource for study and prayer. I have discovered that delving into the spirituality underlying each hymn gives me a clearer sense of my own theological perspective. Often I find that the texts voice my own prayer, like an alternative prayer book. Always, they draw me into God's presence. Giving thoughtful attention to them creates a quiet space of reflection and contemplation.

HOW TO USE THIS BOOK

This book can be used for personal devotion, the preparation of sermons and liturgy throughout the church year, for group study and prayer, and as material for retreats and workshops.

I have used the word "meditating" in the traditional sense of reflecting upon a subject rather than in the more current sense of emptying the mind. The pattern I would suggest for meditating on these hymn texts is adapted from the teaching of St. Ignatius of Loyola:

1. *Preparing.* It is helpful to prepare both physically and spiritually: by settling down in a comfortable position (but not so comfortable you will fall asleep!), centering yourself by paying attention to your breathing, trying to clear the mind of the cares of the day and to focus on the present moment, and quietly offering this time of prayer to God.

The second part of preparation is, of course, to read the text over, either silently or aloud, from *The Hymnal 1982*, or *Poems of Grace: Texts of The Hymnal 1982.*

2. *Picturing.* The first part of each meditation is intended to provide some insight into the writers of the hymns, to point out scriptural allusions in the texts, and to provide other background that will help the words come alive. During this part of the meditation, you are listening in your imagination to the voices who first sang it. When did they live? What did they believe? What were their lives like? You are also listening to the Scripture that so often lies behind these hymn texts, and will wish to have a Bible handy.

3. *Pondering.* Pause before continuing on to this part of the meditation, by sitting in silence for a while and perhaps reading the text over again slowly. In this part of the meditation, you are listening to God speaking to you through the hymn. You are letting the words resonate not merely in your intellect and imagination, but in your heart and will.

What might this hymn mean in terms of your life, your faith, your journey with God? Is there some way in which God might be calling you to respond in a specific way to the messages you hear through this text?

The reflections I have written are intended only to be a catalyst for your own thinking and praying. Do not merely read over what I have written, but give yourself time to plumb the depths of the text on your own.

4. *Gathering*. In conclusion, "gather together" your meditation in any way which you find most helpful. You may wish to write your insights in a journal or in the margins of *Poems of Grace*. You may wish to conclude with your own prayer of gratitude to God for the guidance the hymn provides.

5. *Singing*. Although this book is primarily about the texts of the hymns, this does not mean that we think the music is superfluous. Indeed, what inspired this project is the fact that the music is often so compelling that we neglect to pay adequate attention to the texts. So finally, you may wish to wed words and music by *singing* the hymn, thereby (in the words of Augustine of Hippo), "praying twice."

You may cover the entire pattern of meditating on a hymn during one prayer session. Alternatively, you can extend the project over several days, taking one day, for example, in preparation (reading the hymn and then letting it simmer on your mental "back burner"), one day for "picturing" with the help of the background material; and another for "pondering."

If you say the Daily Offices, you can insert a hymn meditation into Morning or Evening Prayer as a supplementary reading, or add a meditation to Noonday Prayer or Compline.

PREACHING AND LITURGY

If you are responsible for liturgy or preaching, we hope that this book will be a useful resource.

A hymn text associated with the day's lections can provide a fresh approach to preaching, as well as a sensitive and pastoral way to introduce an unfamiliar hymn. The written meditations in this book can be used as a springboard for your own reflection, or you can take the hymn in an entirely different direction. And do not be afraid to ask the congregation to sing at some point during the sermon: you are likely to find new alertness in the pews ever after.

CHRISTIAN EDUCATION

This project was, at the beginning, the result of an assignment in church history class in seminary, in which we were asked to meditate each night on a hymn in *The Hymnal 1982*. I soon found myself drawn into the stories of the poets, saints, martyrs, and quite ordinary people who wrote our hymn texts. Becoming connected with these hymnwriters brought alive to me the eras during which they lived. Hymns not only illustrate periods of church history, however. They also illuminate schools of theology and schools of spirituality as well as providing a lively commentary on Scripture.

QUIET DAYS, RETREATS, AND WORKSHOPS

I have led many quiet days and retreats focusing on hymns, using the meditative pattern—preparing, picturing, pondering, gathering, and singing—and found this pattern to a very effective tool. It engages many aspects of our personalities:

our intellects, because we learn something; our emotions, because not only is our religious fervor kindled but we feel a connection with the writers of the hymns; our physical beings that prefer to sing, and sometimes even to dance, rather than sit still, merely listening; and our spiritual selves, because we find in this endeavor a new means of deepening our knowledge and love of God. With the added resource material found in *We Sing of God: a Hymnal for Children* (Church Publishing, 1989), a similar pattern can be used for intergenerational or children's programs.

Various hymns and their meditations can provide a structure for a program, such as the one I presented during Lent entitled "Ten Ways of Looking at the Passion: A Service of Hymn Meditations."

CONCLUSION

As an addition to the devotional literature of the church, all three books in this series will help both individuals and communities to move towards a new appreciation of the treasure trove that is *The Hymnal 1982*. Its texts are drawn from many denominational sources and historical periods, reflecting the diversity within the Episcopal Church. Like the Book of Common Prayer, *The Hymnal 1982* has been authorized by the General Convention as an expression of our theology and worship, grounded in Scripture, tradition, and reason.

The poetry of our hymns draws us beyond doctrine to faith, and helps us grow in relationship to the mystery of the Holy Trinity, both infinitely beyond us and intimately close to us.

These hymns of almost two millennia are our companions in prayer, helping us to sing in our own hearts the praises of our God:

"So has the Church, in liturgy and song, / in faith and love, through centuries of wrong, / borne witness to the truth in every tongue, / Alleluia!" (Hymn 420, "When in our music God is glorified").

First Sunday of Advent

Hymn 57,58*   Lo! he comes, with clouds descending
Charles Wesley (1707–1788)**

The text of "Lo! he comes, with clouds descending" first appeared in Charles Wesley's *Hymns of Intercession for all Mankind*, published posthumously in Bristol. Designated for the Second Sunday of Advent, it was inspired by an earlier hymn attributed to John Cennick, "Lo! He cometh, countless trumpets."

The first stanza refers to 1 Thessalonians 3:13 ("And may he so strengthen your hearts in holiness that you may be blameless before our God and Father at the coming of our Lord Jesus with all his saints.") and 1 Thessalonians 4:16f. ("For the Lord himself, with a cry of command, with the archangel's call and with the sound of God's trumpet, will descend from heaven, and the dead in Christ will rise first. Then we who are alive, who are left, will be caught up in the clouds together with them to meet the Lord in the air; and so we will be with the Lord forever.")

---

*Hymn numbers throughout this book are from *The Hymnal 1982*.
**For additional biographical information, see *A Closer Walk*, 182–184, *Awake, My Soul!*, 119–120.

Stanza two is inspired by Revelation 1:7: "Look! He is coming with the clouds; every eye will see him, even those who pierced him; and on his account all the tribes of the earth will wail."

The images in stanza three remind the reader of Jesus' post-resurrection appearance to Thomas in John 20:27f. and of the figure of the "Lamb that was slaughtered" in Revelation 6:6–14.

Apocalyptic references to the reign of Jesus from the Book of Revelation continue to permeate the text in stanza four, bringing to a conclusion Wesley's vision of the Second Advent, when Christ will come to receive all his saints in glory and to rule the universe forever.

The text is matched with two popular eighteenth-century tunes.

☙

I love the way the Bible ends:

> See, I am coming soon; my reward is with me, to repay according to everyone's work. I am the Alpha and the Omega, the first and the last, the beginning and the end. . . . It is I, Jesus, who sent my angel to you with this testimony for the churches. I am the root and the descendant of David, the bright morning star. The Spirit and the bride say, "Come." And let everyone who hears say, "Come." And let everyone who is thirsty come. Let anyone who wishes take the water of life as a gift. . . . The one who testifies to these things says, "Surely I am coming soon." Amen. Come, Lord Jesus! The grace of the Lord Jesus be with all the saints. Amen. (Rev. 22:12–21)

In the Book of Revelation, history is over—the long history that began with Genesis: "In the beginning when God created the heavens and the earth, the earth was a formless void and darkness covered the face of the deep, while a wind from God swept over the face of the waters." In the beginning: God.

The beginning of earth's long history, whether told in biblical language (Adam and Eve, the Garden of Eden, Noah, and Abraham) or in scientific language (the Paleozoic, Mesozoic, and Cenozoic eras) was a moment of creation, when the force Christians call God acted to make a planet so intricate and beautiful that humankind can only stand in awe.

Both scientist and prophet know that history thereafter was often a sad tale, for often humankind has disregarded the intricacy and beauty of creation. Our species has destroyed one another, other species, and much of the world fashioned during those first days—or first millennia, depending on how we choose to tell the story.

Apocalyptic literature like the Book of Revelation arose out of this negative view of the world; those who felt powerless in the face of evil found hope in anticipating the end of history, when God would finally intervene. Sometimes this moment was pictured as a day of destruction: "Alas for the day! For the day of the Lord is near, and as destruction from the Almighty it comes."(Joel 1:15)

But destruction does not dominate the Book of Revelation. Instead, biblical history ends with images of fruitfulness and comfort for those who worship before the throne of God and of the Lamb.

And what good person does not worship there? He or she may choose many different ways to express that worship—the way of selflessness, perhaps, or dedication to an art or an ideal, or a passion for the health of the earth. What person does not long for water from the river of life, for fruit from the tree of life, for light in the midst of darkness?

We all long for what the Lord Jesus represents, although we may not all name him in the same way. We all want goodness to reign, rather than evil. We all want history to not have been a waste, but to be gathered up in some eternal purpose—gathered, if you will, into the eternal arms of Love. We are given hope, by the images Charles Wesley gathered into his hymn, that it will be so. That, as "In the beginning: God," so God—and goodness—also will reign in the end.

Second Sunday of Advent

Hymn 69   What is the crying at Jordan?
Carol Christopher Drake (b. 1933)

The poet Carol Christopher Drake was born in Leesburg, Virginia, and educated at Radcliffe College, the University of Washington, and the University of California at Berkeley. Her poetry has appeared in numerous journals and anthologies, and she contributed four texts to *Sing for Joy: A Songbook for Young Children*, edited by Norman and Margaret Mealy.

"What is the crying at Jordan?" was written in the late 1950s, while Drake was a member of the choir of St. Mark's Church in Berkeley.

The poet wrote the text for the tune, of Gaelic origin, which she first discovered in *Sing for Joy*.

 es

A true prophet helps us to look beyond our present preoccupations in order the see the inevitable consequences of our lives. The unkempt John, clad in camel's hair and subsisting on locusts and wild honey, cried out his harsh and hopeful predictions to the crowds who flocked to hear him on the bank of the River Jordan. In that dark season during the reign of Tiberius Caesar, the governorship of Pontius Pilate, and the high-priesthood of Annas and Caiaphas, John attempted to overturn apathy, legalism, and hypocrisy and offer news of the imminent salvation of God. He prepared the way for that salvation by making people feel unsettled. He was not a comfortable person to hear.

Prophets are still unsettling. The message of a true prophet of God continues to be both harsh and hopeful. Almost two thousand years later, the hymnwriter Carol Christopher Drake shows that she is herself one of the lineage of John the Baptist. Salvation was offered to the world by John's cousin Jesus, but Drake notes that human hearts continue to be "dark . . . and shut to mystery." We continue in our apathy, lying down "blind-hearted seeing no light."

We can think about this both on a societal level and on a personal one. On a societal level, an excellent example is the warning from scientists about global warming. Good people, churchgoers, and upstanding citizens alike, really don't want to hear that if global warming continues and the oceans continue to rise, as they are predicted to do, not only some remote Pacific islands—places where we have never traveled and have no friends or family—but New York City and London could someday be under water. This is harsh news, but imbedded in it is the challenge to change the way we run our industries and our automobiles, and therein lies hope. Energized, once we have taken the warnings seriously, we can find new meaning in our work as stewards of God's creation.

On a personal level, have you ever had the experience of not wanting to hear an unpleasant truth about yourself? Perhaps you are in the grip of an addiction, and will not believe it. You busy yourself with distractions, you try to pretend that the reality you are resisting does not exist. Only when you "awake" in the darkness, through God's grace, can a new life dawn.

It was not only at Bethlehem or at Jordan that "joy and terror" were part of the birth of salvation. Terror and joy (probably in that order) continue to be inextricably connected every time we hear the voice of God's prophets, whether they be scientists warning us about climate change or concerned friends confronting us about our habits. We would do well to listen, and to pray, "Lord, give us grace to awake us," for, as Drake reminds us, that is one way that "God gives himself into our lives."

Third Sunday of Advent

Hymn 63,64   O heavenly Word, eternal Light
Latin, ca. 7th cent.

The anonymous Latin hymn *Verbum supernum prodiens* was found in a tenth-century manuscript and in several later sources. In the Roman use, it is assigned to the Office of Readings for Advent.

The hymn addresses Jesus as the Word who brings light to the world. The Word is seen also as fire which purifies the heart, hearkening back to Malachi 3:2:

For he is like a refiner's fire and like fullers' soap; he will sit as a refiner and purifier of silver, and he will purify the descendants of Levi and refine them like gold and silver, until they present offerings to the Lord in righteousness.

The third and fourth stanzas of the hymn are a prayer that our sinfulness not prevent us from seeing the face of Jesus but that we may join the saints in eternal worship, and the concluding stanza is a doxology.

The text is paired with two tunes: a medieval chant found in both France and England and a seventeenth-century German folk song-like melody.

℘

Like the evangelist John, this Latin text addresses the savior who is to come as God's Word and God's Light. It is light that not only illuminates, but purifies "like a refiner's fire."

It is helpful to remember that, until the invention of the electric incandescent light, all illumination, whether from the sun's rays and their lunar reflection, or from oil lamps and beeswax candles, was produced by fire. Therefore, all light produced heat as well.

Many years ago at recess in my elementary school, the big brother of a third-grade classmate naughtily demonstrated this principle by taking a magnifying glass out of his jacket pocket and holding it over my friend's spelling paper until, to our amazement, a scorched circle appeared, finally becoming a full-fledged hole. It haunted me for weeks that the heat from the hot sun far above our school playground destroyed part of my friend's spelling paper.

Fire's power continues to be used, for good as well as for

ill. The home of one of my friends, a concert pianist, was the target of arson; she was away, and when she returned she found her home burned to the ground. She possessed only what was in her suitcase in the trunk of the car. Her clothing and furniture, her Steinway piano, her music, her concert reviews and press releases were gone.

Fire can burn a house, with all the memories it contains, to the ground. But it can also be used to purify. The refiner's fire of which Malachi speaks burns impurities from metals, so that only the precious silver or gold remains. My friend told me later that she actually experienced her house fire this way, although she wouldn't recommend it to anyone. The fire cleared not only some of the cherished possessions in her life, but also much of the debris, and it certainly put what she valued into clearer perspective. She could start anew. "It was like death and resurrection."

So it is with the eternal light and fire of God. As we turn our gaze toward the Word, our hearts can be "fired with ardent love." It is not so much that the Word comes to judge us, but that our love initiates the process of judgment within our very selves. When our souls burn to know God, we become aflame with the desire to purge all within us that separates us from the object of our love, God's own self, as love and penitence become one.

Fourth Sunday of Advent

Hymn 265   **The angel Gabriel from heaven came**
Basque carol; para. Sabine Baring-Gould (1834–1924)

Sabine Baring-Gould was born in Exeter and educated at Clare College, Cambridge, where he immersed himself in the Catholic revival that was in full flower in the Church of England. For several years after he graduated, he taught school and became known for his eccentricities, among them frequently lecturing with a tame bat perched on his shoulder.

Baring-Gould was ordained priest in 1865 and served as curate in the Yorkshire mill town of Horbury, where he fell in love with a sixteen-year-old mill girl named Grace Taylor. He sent her to be educated by friends for two years and paid her parents the equivalent of the wages she would have earned in the mill. In 1868 they were married; the marriage lasted 48 years and produced fifteen children, of whom fourteen lived to adulthood. When Grace died in 1916, he had carved on her tombstone, *Dimidium Animae Meae* (Half My Soul).

In 1871, after a brief stint as curate in the Yorkshire parish of Dalton, near Thirsk, Baring-Gould became rector of East Mersea, Essex. A year later he inherited the family estate in Lew Trenchard, and eventually became rector there (1881), combining the life of a country squire and parson.

Sabine Baring-Gould is most remembered as the author of "Onward, Christian Soldiers," which he always claimed he had dashed off in ten minutes for a procession of school children. But he was a person of many accomplishments, one of the most versatile men of his time.

One writer has likened discovering Baring-Gould to finding the key to a Victorian attic, full of bric-a-brac and treasure. He restored the parish church at Lew Trenchard, revitalized the spiritual life of its two hundred parishioners, and rebuilt its decrepit manor house. He had an affinity with all things old and mysterious, from Nordic sagas to prehistoric stones, and spent happy hours digging in the Bronze Age ruins in Dartmoor. He collected the ballads sung by the old bards of Devonshire into his *Songs of the West*, a project which initiated the rescue from oblivion of English folk song. He was an avid traveler, undertaking long walking tours on the Continent at every opportunity. He produced a sixteen-volume *Lives of the Saints*, containing no fewer than 3,600 biographies. During his long life, he published over one hundred books in fields such as travel, mythology, poetry, fiction, biography, history, and popular theology, among them thirty novels. He was an artist, an opera librettist, and a writer of hymns. He is reported to have had more book titles listed after his name in the literary catalogue of the British Museum than any other author of his time.

In Baring-Gould's *A Book of the Pyrenees* (1907), the author mentions carols from that region; it is likely that both the tune and the text of the Basque carol "The angel Gabriel from heaven came" were recorded by him. Although he himself could not transcribe a tune himself, he generally had it sung to him until he could remember it, and then would have a member of his family write it down for him.

∽

"To me be as it pleaseth God," Mary said. I do not think it was as simple as that.

Mary's acceptance of the angel's message came only at the

end of this encounter between an astonished young woman and a divine messenger. If we look at the account in the first chapter of Luke, we see that her acquiescence was the result of a process.

That process began with fear. After the angel's salutation, "Greetings, favored one! The Lord is with you." Mary "was much perplexed by his words and pondered what sort of greeting this might be." The angel responded, "Do not be afraid."

Gabriel continued with the news that Mary was to bear God's son, and Mary questioned him. "How shall this be, since I am a virgin?" The angel responded with an explanation—"The Holy Spirit will come upon you"—and some reassurance: "Your relative Elizabeth in her old age has also conceived a son. . . . For nothing will be impossible with God."

It was only after Mary had recoiled in fear, and then turned to the angel with her questioning, that she said the words we remember best: "Here am I, the servant of the Lord; let it be with me according to your word."

It is as if there are stations of the Annunciation, similar to the Stations of the Cross that depict the events of Good Friday. They are the "stations" that express the inner movement of Mary's heart as she accepted her vocation.

Ever since I realized this, I have been fascinated with artistic depictions of the Annunciation. In some of them, Mary is drawing back, often with a hand upraised to ward off the awesome presence of the winged creature who has suddenly interrupted her solitude. In others, she has her face upturned in surprise and wonder. In others, she bows with acquiescence.

This is comforting as I struggle with God's various calls to me. It is rarely that I reach the "Here am I, the servant of the

Lord" stage before going through the other two parts of the process.

It is natural to be disturbed when one's best-laid plans are overturned by the sense of a call from God, whether it is the call to a new vocation or simply the hunch that one ought to visit Aunt Suzy in the nursing home today instead of following through with one's carefully thought-out schedule. When God breaks in to our consciousness, in ways great or small, it is a fearful thing, because it makes us realize how thin is the veil between the mundane and the eternal.

It is also natural and healthy to question. "How can this be?" Is it truly God's call, or simply a fantasy? We can not question angelic messengers directly, but God sends us other messengers. We can discuss our dilemma with a trusted friend or spiritual companion. And we can check out our Bibles, to try to discern whether this particular call is in keeping with what we know about God's Good News. In Aunt Suzy's case, for example, we might be reminded by James 1:27 that real religion means to care for widows in their distress.

It is only after we have gone through this process that we are likely to acquiesce to an upheaval in our lives—or schedules.

And I think that God wants it that way. God wants us to respond to the divine calls that come into our lives with that awe which is so close to fear, and also to use our intelligence to reflect on those calls, before we finally answer "yes." Gabriel, in providing patient and loving responses to a frightened, questioning maiden, was truly the emissary of that understanding and compassionate God, who still calls each of us in many ways, and who understands the processes we must go through in order to hear, understand, and accept.

Christmas Day I (Eve)

Hymn 89   It came upon a midnight clear
Edmund H. Sears (1810–1876)

Edmund Sears was born in Sandisfield, a town in the Massachusetts Berkshires, and educated at Union College in Schenectady, New York, and Harvard Divinity School. He served as pastor to Unitarian churches in Wayland, Lancaster, and Weston, Massachusetts. While other classmates from Harvard Divinity School went on to large and influential parishes, he was content to remain in smaller churches, and said in later life, "I had no other ambition than to lead such a quiet pastorate as Goldsmith describes in the *Deserted Village*."[1] Although Sears was a Unitarian, his writing revealed the strong influence of Swedenborg, the Swedish theologian and mystic who emphasized the divine nature of Jesus.

Sears wrote many books, among them his most important book, *The Fourth Gospel* (1872), which was greatly admired in England. His other publications include *Regeneration* (1852), *Pictures of the Older Time* (1857), *Athanasia, or Foregleams of Immortality* (1858), and *Sermons and Songs of the Christian Life* (1875). His name is chiefly remembered today because of this hymn, which is among those published in the *Monthly Religious Magazine*, which Sears co-edited from 1859 to 1871.

"It came upon a midnight clear" was written while Sears was in Wayland. Its text was first published in the *Christian Register* in December 1849. Like many other Unitarian hymns, the text stresses the social implications of the gospel.

At the time Sears wrote, the Civil War was looming on the horizon. It is interesting to note that this Christmas text contains no reference to the birth of Jesus; its focus is, instead, on the message of the angels: "Peace on earth, good will to men."

The text is paired with two tunes in our hymnal. The first, commonly used in the United States, is "Carol," written by a vestryman of the Church of the Transfiguration (New York's "Little Church around the Corner"). The second tune, more common in England, is an adaptation by Arthur S. Sullivan of an English folk melody.

❦

Hear the angels sing! Angels are in vogue. Angel books and angel calendars proliferate on the shelves of gift shops. It makes me wonder what is going on in the national psyche to cause this angelic population explosion.

Like the humans who are so fascinated with these heavenly messengers, these unseen beings depicted by human artists come in all shapes, sizes, ages, and personalities.

Someone has brought me an exquisite small calendar from Italy, entitled *Angeli*. As I turn the pages each month, I realize that most of the angels chosen by the publishers have not grown beyond early childhood and are more akin to cupids than to the celestial hierarchy of Scripture.

Fortunately, these are not the sole representatives of angels in Christian iconography. Angels first flew into the pages of art history in the Byzantine world of the fourth century, serene and serious beings like their classical Greek models. As I turn the pages of a book about angels in art, I see other images, each a product of its time.

I see grieving angels, the hems of their robes blurred like a hummingbird's wings, swooping over the dead Christ being prepared for burial by his mother and disciples. These angels were the spirits of the age as well as of the artist Giotto's imagination, for they expressed the intensity of the four-teenth century's focus on the Passion of Christ. I see numer-ous depictions of the Annunciation, the elegant Gabriels breaking into the enclosed world of the maiden Mary, a favorite theme during the peak of the medieval veneration of the Virgin. On one page is the visionary William Blake's watercolor of two translucent angels guarding the body of Jesus in the tomb, their incorporeal bodies hovering over the corpse like a Gothic arch, suspended in time and space like Blake's mystical poetry.

In all of the images, the angels intersect with human life, signs of God's presence in the world: God's suffering at the Crucifixion, God's sharing in human life at the Annuncia-tion; God's power over death.

The angels of Edmund Sears's hymn, announcing the glorious birth of Jesus to the shepherds on the hill outside Bethlehem, are, like these other angels, a sign of God's pres-ence. Their embodiment as winged beings represents the human attempt to describe the overwhelming sense of the presence not only of God but of heaven itself.

The angels we choose to look upon in our angel calendars and art books may be a barometer of our psyche's need for this presence. What do we seek? I hope that it is not only the self-indulgent comfort brought by the cherubs on my small calendar. Perhaps it is, instead, the compassion of Giotto's winged mourners. Or the challenge of vocation, as in the Annunciations of the Renaissance. Or the promise of a life beyond this one, as in Blake's heavenly beings.

One thing is certain: God's presence, as symbolized by the

angelic host on that clear Christmas midnight, still sings over a weary world. The voices, full of compassion, inspiration, and hope, still call us, because there is still work to do. When we have the vision and imagination to hear them, we will also sing their song: "Peace on the earth, good will to men."

Christmas Day II (Dawn)

Hymn 80   From heaven above to earth I came
Martin Luther (1483–1546) *

It has been said that if Martin Luther had contributed nothing more to the church than his hymns and discerning musical judgment, he would on that account alone deserve to be ranked among the great figures in Christian history.[2] He was an accomplished musician, skilled on the flute and lute and possessing a fine tenor voice. He wrote,

> I am strongly persuaded that after theology, there is no art that can be placed on a level with music; for besides theology, music is the only art capable of affording peace and joy of the heart, like that induced by the study of the science of divinity. A proof of this is that the devil, the originator of sorrowful anxieties and restless troubles, flees before the sound of music almost as much as before the Word of God.[3]

In giving the German people the Bible, the catechism, and the hymnbook in their own tongue, he made it possible

---

*For additional biographical information, see *A Closer Walk*, 83–84.

that "God might speak *directly* to them in His word, and that they might *directly* answer Him in their songs."[4]

The Lutheran liturgist Leupold[5] notes that Luther used an old "garland song" as a basis for the first stanza of this hymn, *Von Himmel hoch da komm ich her*. This popular singing game or "riddle dance" originated in the fourteenth century and was popular in Luther's day. Children would form a circle; then a young man would sing a refrain and give out a riddle to one of the girls in the circle. If she could not solve the riddle, she had to give the singer her wreath or garland. The original garland song, as translated into English by Leupold, reads:

> Good news from far abroad I bring
> Glad tidings for you all I sing,
> I bring so much you'd like to know,
> Much more than I shall tell you though.[6]

For Christmas 1534, Luther re-created this folk song into a narrative nativity drama, very possibly for his own children:

> [Angel]
> From heaven above to earth I come
> to bring good news to everyone!
> Glad tidings of great joy I bring
> of which I must both say and sing;
>
> To you this day is born a child
> of Mary, chosen virgin mild;
> this little child of lowly birth
> shall be the joy of all your earth.
>
> He is our Lord Christ, God from high,
> who hears your sad and bitter cry;

he will himself your Savior be
and from all sin will set you free.

He brings those blessings from above
prepared for you by God in love,
that you shall in his heavenly house
live now and evermore with us.

These are the signs which you should mark
the swaddling clothes and manger stark
there you will find the young child laid
by whom the heavens and earth were made.

[Shepherds]
How glad we'll be to find it so!
Thus with the shepherds let us go
To see what God for us has done
In sending us his own dear Son.

Mark well, my heart, lift up your eyes;
see what within that manger lies?
Who is that lovely little one?
The little Jesus, God's dear Son.

Welcome earth, O noble guest,
through whom this sinful race is blessed!
You come to share my misery.
How thankful I must ever be!

O Lord, who has created all,
how did you come to be so small,
to lie there on the withered grass
provided for the ox and ass?

Were earth a thousand times more fair
and set with gold and jewels rare,
for you it would be much too small,
a narrow cradle, that is all.

For velvets soft and silken stuff
you have but hay and straw so rough
on which, as King so rich and great,
to be enthroned in heavenly state.

Therefore you would make plain to me
the truth which I should clearly see,
that this world's honor, wealth, and might
are vain and worthless in your sight.

O little Jesus, holy child,
prepare a bed, soft, undefiled,
a holy shrine, within my heart,
that you and I need never part.

My heart for very joy now leaps,
my voice no longer silence keeps;
I too must sing with joyful tongue
that sweet and hearty cradle-song:

[All]
Glory to God in highest heaven,
who unto us his Son has given.
With angels sing in pious mirth
a glad new year to all the earth.[7]

The reader can picture one of Luther's children, perhaps
the eight-year-old Hans, singing the part of the angel in stanzas one through five. Other children, along with friends and
guests, would have represented the shepherds, singing stanzas

seven through thirteen while standing around a manger which might have contained Luther's youngest child, Margareta, who was just eight days old on that Christmas Day. Then everyone present would have joined in the final stanza, a paraphrase of the angels' hymn of Luke 2:14.

Although only the first four stanzas, based on the above translation by Catherine Winkworth, were retained in *The Hymnal 1982*, one can still envision this pageant hymn performed by a children's choir and sung to a tune believed to be written by Luther. The melody was later used by J.S. Bach in his Christmas Oratorio and for several of his organ works.

❧

My bishop recently told the story about an incident in one of his parish visitations during the Christmas season. A crèche had been erected near the pulpit for a pageant presented by the church school children. The youngest of them had been designated angels and sat with their parents in homemade costumes until the climatic moment when they were to come forward to sing "Glory to God in the highest, and on earth peace and good will to all people." When the moment arrived, the crèche was soon obliterated from the congregation's view by a solid wall of children clustered close to the figures of Jesus, Mary, Joseph, shepherds, and kings. One very small girl, whose parents had been sitting near the back of the church, was too late to make her way to the front of the angelic crowd. She didn't go back to her parents, nor was she foolish enough to try to shove her way through the older children. Instead, she stood in the middle of the aisle, arms akimbo, and, in stentorian tones, cried out, "Let Jesus show!"

Let Jesus show! Her words rang out, amusing some of the adults in church, no doubt, but certainly becoming food for thought. This passionate and determined child, out of her personal need to see the small figure in the manger scene, ended up challenging everyone in the congregation (including the bishop) to ponder these words for the entire Christmas season, and beyond.

Let Jesus show! For the little girl, that could be easily accomplished: the other children could step aside, parting like the Red Sea, so that the sight line to the crèche could be cleared.

But I am sure that it was not only the bishop who went home and thought what those words *could* mean, outside the church and outside the Christmas season.

First of all, they revealed the little girl's desire to *see* Jesus. Her words articulate the desire of each of us to see the one whom Luther called "the joy of all the earth." We all want Jesus to show! We have an urgent need to know that he hears our prayers, including our "sad and bitter" cries, and that he sets us free from our burdens and our sins. And we are drawn like magnets to the paradox that such a blessing was at one time held in the infant hand of a helpless newborn nestled in a manger.

In the end, however, it is we ourselves who "let Jesus show." For when we do the Christ child's work, we are showing Jesus to the world around us. When we bring the Good News and glad tidings of God's love, when we listen with compassion to the cries of our brothers and sisters and then try to meet their needs, when we ourselves are able to forgive others as God has forgiven us, we are letting Jesus show.

It is as if that tiny infant hand has uncurled and dropped into our own outstretched hands both his blessings and the responsibility of continuing his ministry of "letting Jesus show" in the world around us.

Christmas Day III (Day)

Hymn 102   Once in royal David's city
Sts. 1–2 and 4–6, *Cecil Frances Alexander (1818–1895)**; st. 3,
  James Waring McCrady (b. 1938)

This is one of several hymns written by Cecil F. Alexander for
her Sunday school class during the time she was teaching her
students the Apostles' Creed. It was later published in her
Hymns for Little Children (London, 1848).

  This hymn illustrates the third article of the Creed: "who
was conceived by the Holy Ghost, born of the Virgin Mary."
Like her other hymns written to help her young students
remember the articles of faith ("All things bright and beautiful," written to illustrate "Maker of heaven and earth," and
"There is a green hill far away," explaining "suffered under
Pontius Pilate, was crucified, dead, and buried"), this one is
cherished by children and adults alike.

  The text in *The Hymnal 1982* has been revised from Mrs.
Alexander's original poem, which depicts a vision of childhood that is distinctly Victorian. Susan S. Tamke writes that,
in nineteenth-century children's hymns,

> . . .the child is shown very clearly the virtues which he
> must cultivate to gain a heavenly reward. Chief among
> these virtues are submissiveness and obedience. The
> child is also warned against the temptations of frivolity
> —he must strive for earnestness. In fact, the image of a
> perfect Christian child presented by children's hymns is

---

*For additional biographical information, see *A Closer Walk*, 46–47.

that of a monastic; he is disciplined, he contemplates God continually, he rejects worldly pleasures and he mortifies himself for any transgression.[8]

Therefore, a new third stanza by James Waring McCrady, a linguist and musician, has replaced the following lines by Mrs. Alexander:

> And, through all his wondrous childhood,
>   He would honor and obey
> Love, and watch the lowly maiden,
>   In whose gentle arms he lay;
> Christian children all must be
>   Mild, obedient, good as he.[9]

Because of the extremely high infant and childhood mortality rate of Mrs. Alexander's era, it is not surprising that she closed her hymn with the suggestion that after death, "Like stars his children crowned all in white shall wait around." Tamke writes, "Death is clearly the final goal which these Victorian children are taught to anticipate."[10] In this era of better health care for both young and old, it is appropriate that Alexander's final lines have been replaced, now emphasizing the presence of Christ revealed to all the faithful in heaven.

With its tune, written in 1849 by Dr. Henry Gauntlett, the hymn has become known the world over through the annual Christmas Eve broadcasts of the Service of Nine Lessons and Carols by the choir of King's College, Cambridge.

❧

Every year, on the calendar square marked "Christmas Eve," my husband and I write an appointment: 10:00 A.M.—King's College Chapel. Early that day, we make sure that our radio is tuned to the local public radio station. Sometimes, as 10:00

nears, we even take our phone off the hook. We turn our radio on at least five minutes early. And finally it happens. Over the airwaves comes the disembodied clear voice of one little boy: "Once in royal David's city / stood a lowly cattle shed, / where a mother laid her baby / in a manger for his bed: / Mary was that mother mild, / Jesus Christ her little child."

We wait for that moment all year long. After many visits there, we know King's College Chapel well. On our first visit, we were so overwhelmed with the beauty of the music that we had to take shelter in a side chapel to weep afterwards. We can imagine the dance of the child's voice in the amazing fan vaulting, and the dim light of dusk barely illuminating the stained glass windows. We can see the chapel filled with worshipers; we also have stood in long queues to get into services there.

We can see the choir of lay clerks and boys, wearing their red cassocks and white cottas. And, on Christmas Eve, we can hear them.

What is it about the voice of a boy that is so heart-achingly beautiful? It can be explained, of course, in acoustical or musical terms—something to do with vibrations or overtones. But I think it has to do with more than that. It has to do with our knowledge that this is a sound that will not last; that, one day, this little boy's voice will change and he will be on the way to becoming a tenor or baritone. It has to do with the temporary nature of childhood, and of life itself. The transitory nature of such beauty makes our hearts weep, even as they rejoice.

When such a sound brings us a hymn written for children, with a text describing the birth of a child, the poignancy grows exponentially. No wonder God, after trying to reach God's people through prophets, priests, and sages, finally broke into human time as an infant. God recognized that the power of childhood to rouse our apathy and pierce our cynicism was a mighty weapon of love.

It still is. We have very different views of childhood from the Victorians, but the fact remains that the soul of the child still sings to us of newness and possibility. Looking into the clear eyes of an infant, or hearing a choirboy (or, now, thankfully, a choirgirl as well) refreshes our souls. There is an "otherness" to such innocence; somehow, they seem to us closer to God than we are. One little girl I taught once told me about something that had happened before she was born by beginning, "When I was still with Jesus," and it sometimes does indeed seem as if children *were* someplace else before they came into our human families, and, like Jesus, had "come down to earth from heaven." No wonder that our first celebration of Christmas happens promptly at 10:00 A.M. on Christmas Eve!

First Sunday after Christmas

Hymn 97   **Dost thou in a manger lie**
Jean Mauburn (1460–1503); tr. Elizabeth Rundle Charles (1828–1896) and others

Jean Mauburn was born in Brussels and educated at the cathedral school in Utrecht. He entered the Augustinian monastery at Mont Sainte-Agnès soon after its most celebrated member, Thomas à Kempis, died. Just as Thomas had tried to quicken the piety of the laity through his *Imitation of Christ*, Mauburn hoped to deepen monastic spirituality through his *Rosetum exercitiorum spiritualium et sacrarum meditationum*, which was published in Basle in 1491. The publication of this work not only led to a correspondence between Mauburn and Erasmus, but to a request from Nicolas de Hacqueville, a prominent Parisian canon, that Mauburn come to France to use his gifts to reawaken the spirituality of the monasteries.

He visited five monasteries before being named prior of an abbey at Livry, where he was felled by an illness that treatment in Paris failed to cure.

"Dost thou in a manger lie" is an example of Mauburn's undertaking to develop a prayer discipline that could be used by laity as well as monastics. As St. Ignatius would later do in his *Spiritual Exercises*, Mauburn sought to help his readers focus their thoughts on the Incarnation, and to draw out their feelings about its significance in their personal lives. The hymn originally consisted of thirteen stanzas. In the three chosen for *The Hymnal 1982*, the author notes that the first is intended to evoke "the good will of the listener by compassionate pleading," the second is "The voice of Jesus responding," and the third is "An act of praise arising from the contemplation of the bystanders."[11]

The text is matched with a tune suggested for it by the author.

℘

What a creative way to meditate on Scripture: inventing a dialogue! It is obvious that Mauburn was a gifted pedagogue and spiritual guide; it is no wonder that Canon de Hacqueville summoned him to revivify the dormant spiritual life of the monasteries in France. Often theologians speak of being in conversation with Scripture, but Mauburn shows us exactly how to do it.

Mauburn addressed the infant Jesus in his meditation:

How can it be that you, the creator of all, the long-awaited savior and king, are lying in a manger, poor and without any regal trappings?

The child replies: I am here because I am the only one who can redeem the creation; I willingly take on this lowly birth and life of sacrifice, out of love for you.

The poet concludes with his prayer: Christ, we sing praises of you. We praise the Father for the love of your Son. But only angel voices can praise you adequately, and we join our voices with theirs.

Mauburn's pattern of meditation is simple. First, you choose someone you would like to interview. Next, decide the place and the time. You begin by asking whatever you are wondering about. Then you use your imagination to invent a reply. Finally, in response to that reply, you gather the whole conversation up with your own prayer. Although it is a very simple process, it can be a very profound one.

I, for one, would like to talk with Mary of Bethany, who anointed Jesus' feet with costly perfume made of nard, then wiped them with her hair (Jn. 12:1–11). I have a number of questions for her: "Mary, what made you buy this costly ointment? Was Jesus right when he said you had bought it for the day of his burial? Did you plan to use it in this way far ahead, or was it an impulse? Was it your means, as the quiet sister, to show your love for him? Did it feel like worship? When did you begin to have a perception that he was more extraordinary than any other human being? Did you have any inkling that he was the Son of God? What did the practical Martha say? Did she agree with Judas Iscariot, who questioned your gesture as a waste of money? How did you feel when you heard Judas criticize you? Did that matter?"

What would Mary reply to me? That is where I can let my

imagination have free rein: "I began to realize Jesus' extraordinariness very early, when I sat at his feet, mesmerized by his teaching. (You may remember that I was so mesmerized I neither saw nor heard Martha bustling around in the kitchen.) Then, when Jesus raised my brother Lazarus from the tomb, I knew that his charisma was not just that of a great teacher, but that it came from God. I bought the ointment of nard soon after that; I am not sure why—perhaps because my thoughts about Jesus always led me to the theme of death, and, beyond that, Resurrection. I hadn't planned to anoint his feet until the dinner we had with Lazarus. Then the feeling became overwhelming: I had to pay homage to this man, who brought my brother to life, who brought me to new life every time he looked at me or spoke to me. To tell the truth, I was so caught up in the moment that I didn't even hear Judas and certainly didn't care what Martha thought."

As I am writing, I realize that I have gradually been drawn into the character of Mary by the necessity of imagining what she is thinking. My own part of the dialogue is the following prayer:

> Jesus Christ, may all of my life become adoration. I do not have costly ointment; all I can give you is my thoughts, my prayers, and my actions. May I cherish each moment as if it were precious nard, offered to you and to your brothers and sisters in the world you redeemed.

Second Sunday after Christmas

Hymn 587   Our Father, by whose Name
F. Bland Tucker (1895–1984)*

This hymn was written in 1939 by F. Bland Tucker on the theme of the Christian home. Of its composition, the author writes:

> On the [Joint Commission for the Revision of the *Hymnal*] we were all asked to make a topical index of all the hymns chosen. I wrote down among other topics, "Home and Family," but then discovered that there was no hymn on that topic among those chosen. I looked in other hymnals but could find none (this was 40 years ago), so I tried to write one. I chose the metre 6.6.6.6.8-.8. because there seemed to be more good tunes than words in that metre. I started from Eph. 3:14–15 and then the Trinity suggested the home, parents, children, and the spirit of the family. When the tune *Rhosymedre* was chosen for these words, the last line had to be repeated, so instead I inserted a line of text.[12]

❧

For most people, family life is quite different today than it was in 1939, when F. Bland Tucker wrote this hymn. I was three years old that year. My mother did not work outside the home; instead, she dedicated herself to taking care of our

---

*For additional biographical information, see *A Closer Walk*, 40–41 and *Awake, My Soul!*, 31–32.

neat white house with blue shutters, the flower garden which edged our lawn, and her family. My father left early in the morning to catch the bus to the station, where he boarded a commuter train for New York City. He came home around dinner time; I remember running to fling myself into his arms when I heard him come in the front door each evening. The next year, I asked for a baby brother for my birthday, and, miraculously, my mother actually produced one—on my birthday! Three years later, another brother was born.

We always ate dinner together, gathered around the table in the dining room. Mother was a constant presence in the home. We played informally with the children on the block, mostly outdoors—riding bikes, playing jacks, trading the joker cards from our parents' bridge decks, jump-roping. It was a stable, happy, Norman Rockwell existence.

Some people suggest that a universal return to that kind of family life could be the cure-all of most of our social ills. They warn against the new configurations that family life can take now. They become "moral sentinels," insisting that a family must conform to a certain fixed formula.

But I wonder. Isn't the important thing about the stability and happiness of childhood the fact that "constant love [is] sentinel," not that one particular structure of family life is in place?

Certainly I knew children who also had stay-at-home mothers, fathers who left for the office each day, neat suburban houses surrounded by flower-bordered lawns, but whose families were miserably unhappy. I didn't like going to those homes to play.

I look around at the many families I know today and I still see that some homes are full of love, and some are miserable. There are still some families where each parent fills what used to be the stereotypical gender role: the mother as homemaker, the father as provider. But I know homes where the father is the homemaker and the mother is the breadwinner. I know parents who both manage to tend the home and to work outside the home. I know single mothers and single fathers. I know families divided by divorce, where children move between parents on a regular basis. I know same-sex partners who have undertaken the responsibilities of parenthood. I know parents who live in intentional communities where the child rearing is shared by all the adults in the community.

I cannot agree with the prophets of the doom of "family values" that these new configurations are in themselves dangerous.

For what makes people into family is relationship—not just biological relationship, but a relationship that grows out of living together and loving one another. Like the family of the Trinity—the "Father, by whose Name / all fatherhood is known," the Son, "thyself a child / within an earthly home," and the "Spirit, who dost bind / our hearts in unity"—this relationship is not static: it is dynamic, living, and breathing.

Rather than insisting that our family structures should attempt to replicate an era that cannot be recaptured, we would do well to pray for all parents—of all kinds—and their children, that every home "may be the dwelling place of peace":

> For this reason I bow my knees before the Father, from whom every family in heaven and on earth takes its name. I pray that, according to the riches of his glory, he may grant that you may be strengthened in your inner being with power through his Spirit, and that Christ may dwell in your hearts through faith, as you are being rooted and grounded in love. (Eph.3:14–16)

The Epiphany

Hymn 135   Songs of thankfulness and praise
Sts. 1–3, *Christopher Wordsworth (1807–1885);** st. 4, *F. Bland Tucker (1895–1984)*

This text, which first appeared in Wordsworth's *Holy Year*, is an example of the Wordsworth's project of illustrating the church's theology and liturgical year through hymnody. He imposed upon himself some strict limitations concerning subject matter, seeking his materials only in the Holy Scriptures, in the writings of Christian antiquity, and in the poetry of the ancient church.

The hymnologist John Julian comments that Wordsworth's hymns resemble those of the Eastern church because he interpreted Scripture mystically. Wordsworth wrote that the "frigid and servile modern exegesis of the literalists" was a danger to the faith of England. Instead, he sought the universal *meaning* of the scriptural stories. "The Gospel story was only the history of what 'Jesus *began* to do and to teach' on earth; the Acts of the Apostles and all the Epistles were the history of what he *continued* to do; and the Apocalypse (perhaps his favourite book) was 'the seal and colophon of all.'"[13]

"Songs of thankfulness and praise" was written for use on the Sixth Sunday after Epiphany. Wordsworth described it as

Recapitulation of the successive Manifestations of Christ which have been already presented in the ser-

---

*For additional biographical information, see *A Closer Walk*, 134–135, and *Awake, My Soul!*, 191.

vices of the former weeks throughout the season of
Epiphany, and anticipation of that future great and
glorious Epiphany, at which Christ will be manifested
to all, when he will appear again to judge the world.[14]

The original fourth stanza does indeed speak of the Last
Judgment:

> Sun and Moon shall darkened be,
> Stars shall fall, the heavens shall flee;
> Christ will then like lightning shine,
> All will see his glorious sign:
> All will then the trumpet hear;
> All will see the Judge appear.
> Thou by all wilt be confessed
> God in Man made manifest.[15]

Wordsworth's text is set to a German chant tune harmonized by Johann Sebastian Bach.

&

When I studied history in high school and college, I had a
great deal of difficulty remembering the material. I survived
by cramming before each exam; but I remembered little from
those courses afterwards. I had little interest in politics and
wars, the main focus of the lectures. History certainly did not
come across as a story that had anything to do with my own
life.

It was only when I went to seminary and attended classes
in church history that history began to come alive. Finally,
history became an intriguing story that had an obvious impact upon my own era.

Good teachers know that the human brain has an affinity
for stories. The narratives that my earliest Sunday school

teacher illustrated on an old-fashioned flannel-board are forever embedded in my memory. As children often do, we begged to hear our favorite Bible stories over and over again. (This was also true, of course, of our storybooks at home: my mother always said that if she had been given a penny for every time she read *The Little Engine That Could* to us, she would have become a millionaire.)

Our collection of remembered stories is like an interior library, with books available to us whenever we wish. We can take them off our "internal shelves" and ponder them at leisure.

Christopher Wordsworth's hymns help with the process of learning and remembering. Through the simple language of his hymns, he taught his parishioners the basic stories of their faith. But he always takes these stories to another level, what would have been called in the Middle Ages the "mystical" level: What does this story reveal about God, and what does it have to do with me?

Thanks to the refrain, the reader has no doubt what the "mystical" message is in "Songs of thankfulness and praise." The poet must have been delighted to discover the alliteration and subtle pun of "God in man made manifest." The message is simple: that all the well-loved gospel stories of Jesus' earthly life resonate with deeper meaning. Beyond the narrative lies the ultimate reality: the divine life manifested in a human life.

It is fortunate that none of the books from our interior library become overdue, outmoded, or worn out. For the gospel story needs to be repeated, both to remind us about who Jesus is and to remind us of the source of our life in him. We can read the book of "God in man made manifest" our whole lives long, always discovering new mystery and new meaning.

First Sunday after Epiphany

Hymn 139   When Jesus went to Jordan's stream
Martin Luther (1483–1546)*; para. F. Bland Tucker (1895–1984)

Luther's hymns fall into five categories: translations from Latin, hymns based on Pre-Reformation popular hymns, versions of psalms, paraphrases of other portions of Holy Scripture, and original hymns, of which *Christ unser Herr sum Jordan kam* ("When Jesus went to Jordan's stream") is an example. This is the last of the hymns that Luther wrote on the five main parts of his catechism:

Ten Commandments: *Dies sind die heilgen zen Gebot*
Creed: *Wir glauben all an einen Gott*
Lord's Prayer: *Vater unser im Himmelriech*
Baptism: *Christ unser Herr zum Jordan kam*
Eucharist: *Jesus Christus, unser Heiland, der von uns*

The heading of this hymn on baptism—"A Spiritual Song of our Holy Baptism, which is a fine summary of what it is, who is established by it, and how it is to used, etc."—resembles a summary of the respective section in his *Short Catechism*, published in Wittenberg in 1529. The *Short Catechism*, unlike Luther's *Long Catechism* (intended as an instruction manual for Christian teachers) was intended for catechumens—people who were just learning the faith.

Luther's chorales were intended to proclaim a message: the Good News of the Gospel. Their melodies were sung in

---

*For additional biographical information, see *A Closer Walk*, 83–84.

unaccompanied unison by the people, often alternating with polyphonic settings sung by the choir. This was especially true in the *de tempore* hymn, or hymn of the day, which was appointed to be sung between the Epistle and the Gospel.

Luther, in the tradition of the Meistersingers who composed their own music for their poems, emphasized the unity of melody and text. His vigorous and strong chorales underscore the gospel message he wished to proclaim.

∽

I have discovered a wonderful resource for meditation. It is a series of three arts and lectionary resources called *Imaging the Word* published by the United Church Press.[16] The poetry, short quotations, and illustrations in these volumes provide new material which help me explore the themes of the faith. Like the hymns in *The Hymnal 1982*, they harken from many centuries, places, and peoples.

Among the offerings for the First Sunday of Epiphany are several depictions of the baptism of Jesus, each of which helps me see the event through another's eyes. They can also serve as illustrations of the text of Luther's hymn.

"God is thus made known / in Christ as love unending." The earliest depiction of Jesus' baptism in *Imaging the Word* is one of the famous mosaics created for the dome of the Baptistery in Ravenna, Italy, about fifteen hundred years ago. It shows a naked Christ standing in the Jordan. John the Baptist pours water over him from a bowl and a figure awaits the ceremony's completion with a cloth extended towards Jesus for his use. I remember seeing this mosaic in a slide shown by my church history professor, who explained that this particular depiction of the baptism, with the human body so clearly represented, accentuated Jesus' humanity at a time when the controversies

about Jesus' human and divine natures were in progress.[17]

 "And till God's will is fully done / he will not bend or waver."
A contemporary painting by North American artist Pheoris
West depicts a strong black Jesus with his face both turned
toward John and confronting the viewer, in the manner,
although not the style, of cubism. The artist shows the moment of centered commitment, as Jesus begins his ministry
of teaching and healing.[18]

"Then let us not heed worldly lies." A photograph by W.
Eugene Smith called "Tomoco in Her Bath" shows a mother
gently bathing a deformed child. The caption tells me that it
was published in 1972 in *Life* magazine and "caused an
international outcry against the industrial polluters whose
careless environmental policies led to the severe birth defects
suffered by Tomoko."[19]

"He came by water and by blood / to heal our lost condition."
The final illustration, a serigraph by John August Swanson
entitled "The River"[20] gathers together the themes in the
others. It is a tall picture, with a river beginning in the distance at the top and flowing toward the observer. Along the
banks of the river are vignettes of human life: farmers working in the fields, a shepherd tending his sheep, women wash-
ing their clothes, women with water jugs, children swim-
ming. The river is the river of human life, and Jesus has
plunged right into it. In the foreground, he kneels in the
water. Beside him is John, baptizing him from a bowl reminiscent of the Ravenna mosaic. Above their heads is a dove
from which light streams down upon them.

Jesus has entered the river of life in which we too live. His
baptism assures us of this truth: that we can trust in the
*"Christ who will baptize / with water and the Spirit / that we
may life inherit."*

Second Sunday after Epiphany

Hymn 333   Now the silence
Jaroslav J. Vajda (b. 1919)

The Lutheran pastor Jaroslav Vajda was born in Lorain, Ohio. His childhood was spent in a home where the traditions and language of his Slovak forebears were maintained. He was educated at Concordia College in Fort Wayne, Indiana and Concordia Seminary, St. Louis, Missouri, and received a honorary L.L.D. from Concordia College, Seward, Nebraska, in 1987. During his years of ministry, he served parishes in Pennsylvania and Indiana, some of them bilingual (Slovak and English). He was editor of *The Lutheran Beacon* of the Evangelical Lutheran Church, was editor of *This Day* magazine, and book editor and developer for Concordia Publishing House in St. Louis.

Although he had begun writing poetry at the age of eighteen, it was after his retirement that Vajda became active as a hymnwriter. Known as the "the poet laureate of the Lutheran Church,"[21] he is also known for his workshops dealing with the craft of hymnody. Vajda's book *Now the Joyful Celebration* (St. Louis, 1987), contains his reflections on hymnwriting as well as texts of both original hymns and translations. His Slovak upbringing and his study of classic languages while at seminary provided skills for his work as translator of hymns and literature of his own heritage.

In his foreword to *Now the Joyful Celebration*, Carl Schalk writes that Vajda's "vocation as pastor and preacher and later as editor and book developer, helped to hone the skills necessary to both the translator's and hymnwriter's art: clarity of imagery and the ability to convey that imagery with economy and power."[22] He identifies three important qualities of Vajda's writing: "The ability to fashion a striking new image, or to reshape an older image . . . ; his affinity for less usual textual forms and meters . . . ; and the strong theological thrust of his texts."[23]

Vajda himself writes,

> Why then do I write hymns? To stir up my own awareness of God's will and mercy, to express my own need for him and to begin to render some genuine appreciation for his love, to review my place in his plan for me and for humanity, to refresh myself with his love so as to be able to feed others with it, to experience his forgiveness so that I can forgive others, to taste his peace so that I can be its instrument to others still at war with him, with themselves and one another and to look forward to God's ultimate goal for me, for which I have been redeemed at so great a cost.[24]

This hymn grew out of the first phrase of a sonnet by Pavol Orszá Hviedzdoslav (1849–1921), Slovakia's greatest poet: "Wish me silence, wish me peace." The text was inspired by Habakkuk 2:20 ("But the Lord is in his holy temple; let all the earth keep silence before him!") and Psalm 122:1 ("I was glad when they said to me, 'Let us go to the house of the Lord!'").

Vajda has stated that although the hymn was quickly written, it took many years of thought and prayer before he was ready to commit it to paper:

> The hymn text originated while I was shaving one morning (a time when I get a lot of original ideas). Since my teenage years I have been writing and translating

poetry, so many poetic phrases run through my mind, some of them ending up on paper. Somewhere in the back of my mind, during my previous eighteen years in the full-time parish ministry, I was accumulating reasons and benefits in worship. I have felt that we often get so little out of worship because we anticipate so little, and we seldom come with a bucket large enough to catch all the shower of grace that comes to us in that setting. Suddenly the hymn began to form in my mind as a list of awesome and exciting things one should expect in worship, culminating in the Eucharist and benediction.... Subconsciously I was producing a hymn without rhyme or without worn clichés, depending entirely on rhythm and repetition to make it singable. The reversal of the Trinitarian order in the benediction was made not only to make the conclusion memorable, but to indicate the order in which the Trinity approaches us in worship: The Spirit brings us the Gospel, by which God's blessing is released in our lives.[25]

This sensitive, impressionistic eucharistic text is matched by a tune written in 1968 for use with the Vajda text by the Lutheran church musician Carl Schalk.

∽

Now. Now. Now. Great spiritual guides of every religion tell us that our life in the present moment is one of God's greatest gifts. There are teachings from every tradition to help us to set aside past worries and future anxieties in order to enjoy this gift. Learning the importance of "now" is especially appropriate when it comes to our time with God, whether in private prayer or in worship.

How often have we set aside time for private contemplation of God and found ourselves mentally drawing up our grocery shopping list instead? At church, how often have we been sidetracked from the liturgy by wondering just why the person across the aisle thought that particular outfit was attractive? It is often difficult to settle down to simple attentiveness to God amid the myriad distractions that take our busy minds elsewhere.

Jaroslav Vajda's hymn text helps us focus on *now*. First, it is quiet and introverted. Try hearing the music and words in your mind and just breathing to its relaxed rhythm. This attention to breathing is an important tool for living in the present. Inhalation and exhalation recall us to our body's experience of time, releasing us from the frantic pace of the world around us. Quiet breathing helps us shed our tensions, both physical and mental, so that we can be open to God.

Focusing on our breathing in church or at prayer helps us enter into silence. There still may be noise around us—the lawnmower or snowblower outside our window, or the chatter of children sitting beside their parents in the pews— but our spirits become quiet.

When we have settled down into a focused silence, we notice in a new way everything that happens around us. Vajda helps us to notice, by pointing out some of those moments in the liturgy that have become mere habit because we have experienced them so often: our empty hands uplifted to receive the bread at communion; the pleading prayer that the body expresses when it is kneeling; the power of the words we hear; the dark red wine poured from the cruet into the chalice.

When we are quiet enough within ourselves to focus on the liturgy like that, we live in God's *now*. We have stepped out of the world's time and entered heavenly time, an eternal present. And we find that our hearts leap with joy, as we celebrate this liturgy which unites us again and again to our God. Now. Now. Now.

Third Sunday after Epiphany

Hymn 536   God has spoken to his people
Willard F. Jabusch (b. 1930)

This hymn brings the spirit of Hasidic Judaism to *The Hymnal 1982*. Hasidic Judaism was a revival movement which began in the eighteenth century. Its leader the Ba'al Shem Tov and his followers sought to bring new life to religious practice. They viewed all of Jewish life as service to God. Study, deeds of human kindness, and worship alike were for God's sake, the fulfillment of the desire implanted within the human soul for a return to its original state of oneness with God.

> The mystical ecstasy of Hasidism flows from the rediscovery that God is present in all of human life. All things and all moments are vessels that contain the Presence .... Hasidism thus teaches that all of life is an extension of the hour of prayer, and that prayer itself is the focal point around which one's entire day is centered.[26]

"Open your ears, O faithful people," deeply rooted in the imagery of Hebrew Scripture and imbued with the spirit of Hasidism, is by Willard F. Jabusch, a Roman Catholic priest who has training both in music and in theology. He was educated at Chicago's Loyola University and the Chicago

Conservatory of Music, the University of London, Tantur Ecumenical Center in Israel, and the Mexican American Cultural Center, San Antonio. After serving in various parishes, he turned to teaching, holding the John S. Marten chair of Liturgics and Homiletics at Notre Dame. His most recent position was as professor of Homiletics and chair of the Ministry Department at St. Mary of the Lake Seminary in Mundelein, Illinois.

Jabusch has authored several books on homiletics and hymnody, including *The Person in the Pulpit*, *A Heritage of Hymns*, *Walk Where Jesus Walked*, *Singing His Story*, and *Songs of God*. He wrote the book and lyrics for the musical *Francesco* and for a musical based on the life of Vincent de Paul, and has published over two hundred hymns in various languages. He is skilled in using religious language that is both poetic and easily accessible.

This melody is one of a large number of melodies in "Hasidic style" written in a mode that assumed a prominent place in the synagogue music of Eastern Europe, as well as in Jewish folk music.

ↄ

When Hasidic Judaism is mentioned, what comes to your mind? I would guess that you would visualize black-garbed, bearded men with long strands of hair at their temples. It is also likely that this would be not a static but a fluid image, like the sculpture of a Hasid I once saw in an art exhibit at a synagogue—it actually could be set in motion with the touch of a hand so that it davened, or bowed, repeatedly. Hasids are often in motion, davening as they pray, or dancing ecstatically.

These outward manifestations of movement flow from the belief that God is present in all of human life. "All things and all moments are vessels that contain the Presence." The integration that this brings to the spirit of the devout erases the separation between body and spirit that is an all too common aspect of contemporary practice.

Instead of sitting quietly as you read a meditation about this lively hymn, perhaps you should emulate the Hasids, and get up and dance! You can do this alone, or gather your family and friends together in a circle. Whichever you choose, you will discover the true spirit of the *Torah Song*, the song in which worshipers celebrate the word of God in the Pentateuch (the first five books of our Bible) with so much joy that they literally get up and dance with the scrolls.

Ready?

Here is the simple version of a *Torah Dance*:

1. Take a step to your right, then bring your left foot alongside.
2. Do this again.
3. Then step right and give a little hop on the right foot as you kick your left foot forward in front of your right foot.
4. Step left and give a hop as you kick your right foot forward in front of your left foot.
   Continue repeating this pattern throughout the hymn.

After you have mastered this, you may wish to substitute the grapevine step for the first two parts:

1. Step right and cross your left foot in front of you, putting your weight entirely on the left foot.
2. Step right and cross your left foot behind you, putting your weight entirely on the left foot.
3. As above.
4. As above.

Whichever pattern you choose, and whether you are thinking of the melody or just of the rhythm of the words, you will be repeating these movements six times for each stanza of the hymn.

However, in order to truly experience the spirit of Hasidism, you need to go beyond remembering steps. You will need to experience your body's energy and your increased need to breathe as a prayer. It is a prayer of celebration that God is present in the Scripture, but also present in your body as well as your spirit, and in every moment of your daily life. Hallelujah!

Fourth Sunday after Epiphany

Hymn 694   God be in my head
Sarum Primer, 1514

"God be in my head" first appeared in manuscript form in a 1514 *Book of Hours*, a collection of prayers for use at designated times during the day. It was later included in the 1541 Sarum Primer *Hore beate marie/virginis ad usum in/ signis ac preclare ec/clesie Sarum*, a prayer book used in Salisbury, England. The text became very popular in its day and was included as a prayer to be said before the daily offices in Archbishop Cosin's *Collection of Private Devotions*. It was also published in French collections of prayers.

The text became well known to present-day Anglicans through its use in a short anthem setting by Sir Walford Davies. It first appeared as a hymn text in *The Oxford Hymn Book* of 1908, where it was also used as a motto for the volume. The hymnologist Percy Dearmer called it a "modest little jewel" in his *Songs of Praise Discussed.*[27]

The text is set to a meditative tune in simple ABABA form by a former organist of Westminster Abbey.

❧

I have always been struck by this text that brings together our intellectual, emotional, and spiritual lives so well. Most people would have written, "God be in my head, and in my thinking. . . . God be in my heart, and in my understanding." But not the writer of this "modest little jewel"!

The prayer reminds me of the nineteenth-century Russian Bishop Theophan the Recluse, who spoke of the act of prayer as "standing before God with the mind in the heart." In his view, prayer helps the rational part of us to descend into the heart, the part of us that feels and wills and makes decisions.

Knowledge without understanding has been responsible for many disasters throughout human history. Inebriated with our inventions—the atom bomb, D.D.T., the internal combustion engine, thalidomide—it is only later that we wish we had tried to understand—before we used them—how they might change our world.

Yet the reverse is true as well: we cannot really understand without knowledge. The great environmental challenge of this new century requires us to learn everything we can about the intricate web connecting nature and society. For example, we may wish with all our hearts that poverty could be alleviated in Central America, and yet not realize that we contribute to it when we buy products grown by great corporations on land that once supported its native peoples. Some very good and well-intentioned people do things that contribute to the potential destruction of various forms of life on this planet, merely from ignorance.

To keep up with such issues sometimes seems an endless and often depressing task, but it seems to me that it is an ingredient of what "goodness" means in our time. If we substitute that word "goodness" for "God" in the prayer from the *Sarum Primer*, the point will be clear.

"Goodness be in my head, and in my understanding; / Goodness be in mine eyes, and in my looking; Goodness be in my mouth, and in my speaking; / Goodness be in my heart, and in my thinking; / Goodness be at mine end, and at my departing." As life in this world changes, what goodness means in terms of behavior changes.

It is sometimes difficult to keep up with such rapid adjustments in the way we think and act. But surely the One who is Eternal Goodness calls us to do so, and to open our minds and our hearts, our eyes and our speech, to God's divine guidance.

Fifth Sunday after Epiphany

Hymn 671   Amazing grace! how sweet the sound
John Newton (1725–1807); st.5, from *A Collection of Sacred Ballads, 1970*; compiled by *Richard Broaddus* and *Andrew Broaddus*.

Born in London, the son of a shipmaster and a mother who died when he was seven, John Newton was largely self-taught, having received no formal education beyond two years of school in Stratford, Essex. (When he was sixty-seven, however, he received an honorary Doctor of Divinity from the College of New Jersey, now Princeton University.)

Newton went to sea with his father when he was only eleven. His life at sea was full of reckless escapades, but eventually he became the master of a slave ship. His reading of the Bible and the *Imitation of Christ* by Thomas à Kempis prepared the way for a conversion during a storm at sea.

He left the slave trade to become tide surveyor in Liverpool (1755–1760), during which time he became acquainted with Whitefield, Wesley, and the Nonconformists. He prepared for ordination, studying Hebrew and Greek and reading theology. When the Archbishop of York refused to ordain him, Newton spent several years trying to find openings in the Anglican ministry. Ultimately, the curacy of Olney in Buckinghamshire was offered to him, and he was ordained in 1764 by the Bishop of Lincoln.

In Olney, he became friends with the poet William Cowper. Together they published *Olney Hymns* (London, 1779), to which Newton was the major contributor. The volume was an important and influential expression of the evangelical movement of the late eighteenth century. The hymnologist John Julian writes of Newton's hymns: "his rich acquaintance with Scripture, knowledge of the heart, directness and force, and a certain sailor imagination, tell strongly."[28]

In 1780, Newton was appointed rector of St. Mary's, Woolnoth, in the city of London, where he attracted a large congregation. During the latter part of his life, he was active in the anti-slavery movement, collaborating with William Wilberforce and Josiah Wedgwood. In 1805, when he was no longer able to read his sermon text and it was suggested that he discontinue preaching, he replied, "What, shall the old African blasphemer stop while he can speak!"[29] He lived just long enough to hear the news that Parliament had abolished the British slave trade in 1807.

Newton wrote his own epitaph:

John Newton clerk
once an Infidel and Libertine
A servant of slaves in Africa
was by the rich mercy of our Lord and Saviour
Jesus Christ
Preserved, restored, pardoned
And appointed to preach the Faith
He had long laboured to destroy.[30]

"Amazing grace" was written sometime before 1779. It is based on King David's questioning prayer in 1 Chronicles 17:16: "Who am I, O Lord God . . . that you have brought me thus far?" Like other hymns by Newton, the text is autobiographical, alluding to the degraded way of life he had led in the slave trade and his conversion and gratitude for the guiding hand of God.

Newton did not use the word "wretch" lightly. *Olney Hymns* contains at least ten other examples of the term, used to describe the human condition before receiving God's grace. "Wretch" is more than autobiographical: it is part of the "theological vocabulary" of Newton's hymns, enshrining the poet's understanding of the universal truth of salvation.

The final stanza is an example of a "wandering stanza" that appears at the end of a variety of hymns in nineteenth-century hymnals.

Robin A. Leaver writes,

This is a truly remarkable hymn. It has been translated into many different languages and adapted into a multitude of different cultural styles. There is an incredible poignancy in the fact that the author, John Newton, was once a slave ship captain and that this hymn continues to be sung with intensity by the descendants of those who were shipped as cargo in slave ships like Newton's, as well as by descendants of the ship's owners.[31]

The pentatonic tune associated with the poem has appeared with the text in American hymn collections for more than one hundred and fifty years.

∽

Amazing grace! I am not the only person who from time to time suspects that the sight of privileged Christians with high self-esteem singing about "a wretch like me" borders on comedy. But when John Newton's text is illuminated by his biography, his hymn becomes a challenge instead of merely a comfortable opportunity to bask in temporary humility.

God's amazing grace changed Newton's life. It is as simple as that. The high seas were for Newton what the Damascus road was to St. Paul, who wrote after his own conversion, "I am the least of the apostles, unfit to be called an apostle, because I persecuted the church of God. But by the grace of God I am what I am, and his grace toward me has not been in vain." (1 Cor. 15:9–10) Newton's blindness to the humanity of his African cargo paralleled Paul's blindness to the humanity of the Christians he persecuted. Once his eyes were opened, it was impossible for life to continue as before.

That is something many of us overlook, as we sway to this popular hymn, with its rocking motion of comfort and assurance. God's grace is "costly"; it is so valuable that we should be challenged and inspired to respond. As Dietrich Bonhoeffer wrote:

Cheap grace means grace sold on the market like cheapjack's wares. The sacraments, the forgiveness of sin, and the consolations of religion are thrown away at cut prices. Grace is represented as the Church's inexhaustible treasury, from which she showers blessings with generous hands, without asking questions or fixing limits. Grace without price, grace without cost! The essence of grace, we suppose, is that the account has been paid in advance; and, because it has been paid, everything can be had for nothing. . . .

Cheap grace means the justification of sin without the justification of the sinner. Grace alone does everything, they say, and so everything can remain as it was before. . . . Instead of following Christ, let the Christian enjoy the consolations of his grace! That is what we mean by cheap grace. . . . [32]

God's amazing grace challenges me, just as it confronted St. Paul, John Newton, and Dietrich Bonhoeffer. When I sing Newton's hymn, I am reminded that it will take the rest of my life to respond.

Sixth Sunday after Epiphany

Hymn 339   Deck thyself, my soul, with gladness
Johann Franck (1618–1677); tr. Catherine Winkworth
(1827–1878)***

This classic German Lutheran eucharistic text by Johann
Franck first appeared in the author's *Hundert-Thönigue
Vater-Unsers-Harffe*, published in Wittenberg in 1646, where
the first line, *Schmücke dich, O liebe Seele* was cited. Three
years later, a single stanza appeared in print, along with
Johann Crüger's magnificent melody. Eight more stanzas
were added in the fifth edition of Crüger's *Praxis Pietatis
Melica*, published in Berlin in 1653. Later, in his 1674 vol-
ume *Geistliches Sion*, Franck gave it the title "Preparation for
Holy Communion."

The text is typical of the devotional poetry emphasizing
the relationship between the individual and Jesus so characteristic of the period during and after the devastation of the
Thirty Years War (1618–1648). It has been suggested that
Franck's poem was influenced by Thomas Aquinas's eucharistic hymn, *Lauda Sion Salvatorum*, (see Hymn 320), which
also consists of lines of eight syllables.

The translation is based on that of Catherine Winkworth
in *The Chorale Book for England* (1858). One of the church's
most beloved eucharistic hymns, it was included in *The*

---

*For additional biographical material, see *A Closer Walk*, 151–152.
**For additional biographical material, see *A Closer Walk*, 84–85 and
Awake, My Soul!,13.

Hymnal 1940, reflecting the historical bond between Lutherans and the Church of England and responding to the growing ecumenical movement.

The poem is matched with Crüger's beautiful chorale
setting written especially for Franck's text.

∽

In Jesus' parable of the marriage feast in Matthew's gospel,
there is a "coda" about the arrival of a "man who had no wedding garment." (Matthew 22:11) I'd always wondered what
that wedding garment might be like, until I began to ponder
the text of Johann Franck's beautiful eucharistic hymn. The
poet gives me the answer: the "wedding garment" we are to
wear at the wedding banquet in eternity, as well as in the
celestial banquet on earth that is the Eucharist, is the garment
of gladness.

I think that most of us have had the experience of arriving
at an event and realizing we were dressed inappropriately. I
went to college during the late 1950s in a small Midwestern
town; when we were invited to a dance, we wore strapless tulle
gowns reaching almost to the floor, often with a wisp of additional tulle over our shoulders; on the dance floor, we all
looked like members of a *corps de ballet*. Soon after I graduated
and returned to my home town in the New York suburbs, I
was invited to a party for recent college graduates at the local
Woman's Club. Happily decked in my finery, I arrived at the
party site only to find that eastern fashions had changed in my
absence, and that the other women were wearing sophisti-
cated cocktail dresses. Dancing in my full gown, which had
previously made me feel like a princess, now made me feel like
Mrs. Rip Van Winkle, uneasy in this room full of contemporaries who were, unlike me, up to date.

I see examples of this kind of thing occasionally in the concerts we attend here in our musical college town. Once in a while, someone does not get the message. Everyone in the chorus wears black, with the exception of the alto who forgot, and stands radiant in a white blouse and dark skirt. Or every orchestral player has agreed to wear informal concert clothes, except for the oboist who did not pay attention and arrives in a tuxedo.

Wearing the wrong clothing creates some momentary embarrassment. But how about our souls? In the coda to Jesus' parable about the wedding feast, the consequences are more dire: not temporary humiliation but eternal exile!

What is the soul's clothing code in the Eucharist, that meal which is a foretaste of the celestial wedding banquet? And what kind of clothing is inappropriate, or makes us feel as if we do not fit in?

If I had had access to a video link with the Woman's Club on that day so many years ago, I would have been able to observe the other women there and to realize that my dress would not have fit in. If the alto and the oboist had similar technology, they would not have been the unintentional, though brief, focus of the audience's amused attention.

But we can "see" the other guests at God's banquet before we get there. We gather there, at the altar, in the company of the communion of saints, those blessed ones who know that the kingdom of God belongs to the poor, and that at God's table the hungry are satisfied and the sorrowful are able to laugh. Those blessed ones know that even being excluded from human society can never dilute their joy, and that no one is ever turned away from this gathering of God's guests because of what they are wearing.

The only ones who are uncomfortable there are the ones

whose souls are decked with attire—like hatred, greed, and violence—that became out-of-date the instant the Good News was proclaimed. The only way to fit in to this party is to leave those old styles behind and to choose a new wardrobe: the gladness of the daylight's splendor, wondrous joy, and gratitude overflowing like a fountain because we are God's beloved guests.

Seventh Sunday after Epiphany

Hymn 304   I come with joy to meet my Lord
*Brian A. Wren (b. 1936)**

Brian Wren is an English hymnwriter, theologian, and activist for world development, who wrote this hymn in 1968 for his congregation at Hockley, Essex, "to sum up a series of sermons on the meaning of communion."[33] Stanza one begins with the individual worshiper ("I come with joy to meet my Lord") and then moves, in the second stanza, into the corporate dimension of the Eucharist ("the new community of love in Christ's communion bread"). The third stanza begins with the image of Christ himself breaking the bread for us, bidding us share it as we reconcile those things which divide us. In the fourth stanza, Wren suggests that it is not only in the bread that we find Christ's presence, but also in this new friendship with strangers, forged at the altar. The hymn ends in the spirit of the dismissal in the Eucharist, as

*For additional biographical information, see *Awake, My Soul!*, 206–207.

this community, "together met, together bound" goes its separate ways.

The text is set to an American folk hymn.

ɤ

Most of us are familiar only with the parish churches in which we have worshiped; we have little opportunity to gain perspective on the faith and practice of the church at large. By coincidence, I write this meditation shortly after I have returned from a conference where there was a presentation on the Zacchaeus Project, an initiative of the Episcopal Church Foundation. Like Zacchaeus, who climbed up a tree growing beside the dusty road to Jericho in order to have a better view of Jesus, the project bearing his name attempts to give us a better view of what it means to be an Episcopalian today.

Among the major findings of the research undertaken by the Zacchaeus Project was the universal centrality of worship —in particular the weekly celebration of the Eucharist—in the Episcopal tradition. "As with Zacchaeus, Christ comes to have meals with us as we are, and being in His presence changes our life."[34]

The Eucharist has not always been central in the Episcopal Church on Sunday mornings. Sunday worship in my childhood and youth usually meant Morning Prayer, with its sung *Venites*, *Te Deums*, and *Benedicites*. During the past century, new insights into the importance of baptism and the Eucharist were embodied in what some still call the "new" prayer book (almost a quarter of a century old at this writing!) And we are not the only denomination in which the Eucharist has moved into a more prominent place in worship.

Morning Prayer has not by any means disappeared. A group of faithful parishioners gathers every weekday morning in my own parish church to say Morning Prayer and hold the needs of the community before God, and I know many clergy and laity who make a practice of praying both Morning Prayer and Evening Prayer privately at home. But on Sunday morning, the real happening occurs: we come with joy to meet our Lord in a meal.

"As Christ breaks bread and bids us share, / each proud division ends," writes Brian Wren. We often wish that were so. The reality is that there is a great deal of disagreement in the Episcopal Church today—another discovery of the Zacchaeus Project, and one which most of us knew already. Our disagreements are in part a result of the church's long tradition of embracing diversity. Within one congregation, there are likely to be people of many cultural and religious backgrounds, and certainly of many generations. We not only "go our different ways" literally, as we walk out the church door after the Eucharist; we often "go our different ways" in matters of ethics and theology.

So what glue holds us together? We certainly do not look alike, or act alike, or even, sometimes, believe alike.

What keeps us together is, in fact, food: the bread and the wine. When we gather at the altar on Sunday mornings, we enter a realm that transcends our earthly disagreements. For these few moments, our proud divisions can be forgotten. We are in a place beyond argument, beyond logic, beyond belief itself. At the altar, we don't discuss God's love, or reason it out, or decide who deserves it.

We—all of us—partake of it.

Eighth Sunday after Epiphany

Hymn 597   O day of peace that dimly shines
Carl P. Daw, Jr. (b. 1944)

Carl P. Daw, Jr. was born in Louisville, Kentucky and educated at Rice University, the University of Virginia, and the University of the South. He was assistant professor of English at the College of William and Mary in Williamsburg, Virginia, before his ordination to the Episcopal priesthood. He served churches in Petersburg, Virginia and Storrs, Connecticut. He is now the Executive Director of the Hymn Society of the United States and Canada and is on the faculty of Boston University.

Regarded as one of the most gifted of contemporary American hymnwriters, he was on the Text Committee of the Standing Commission on Church Music (SCCM), which took a major role in preparing *The Hymnal 1982*. His hymns are collected in *A Year of Grace: Hymns for the Church Year* (1992) and *To Sing God's Praises: 18 Metrical Canticles* (1992) and are also found in many major denominational hymnals.

"O day of peace that dimly shines" was composed in response to two special requests received by the SCCM. First, the General Convention's Joint Commission on Peace urged that the hymnal contain a number of hymns on the theme of world peace. The second came from many sources: the request that the stirring tune "Jerusalem" by the British composer Charles Hubert Hastings Parry be included in the hymnal.

Daw played "Jerusalem" over and over on a variety of instruments for a number of days, but no text came. He finally decided to set aside the project for awhile and to catch up on some neglected reading. He began to read *Turning to Christ* by Urban T. Holmes III. On page 25, Holmes quoted Isaiah 11:6–8:

> The wolf shall live with the lamb,
> the leopard shall lie down with the kid,
> the calf and the lion and the fatling together,
> and a little child shall lead them.
>
> The cow and the bear shall graze,
> their young shall lie down together;
> and the lion shall eat straw like the ox.
>
> The nursing child shall play over the hole of the asp,
> and the weaned child shall put its hand on the adder's den.

Daw recognized that the passage (which continues with "They will not hurt or destroy on all my holy mountain; for the earth will be full of the knowledge of the Lord as the waters cover the sea") held the heart of the hymn he was trying to write.

Holmes had died suddenly only a few months before and had been one of the great influences on Daw during his years as a seminarian at the School of Theology at the University of the South.

Daw began with writing the second stanza, a paraphrase of the Isaiah passage. The first stanza then evolved as a prayer for the peaceful existence described by Isaiah. Daw himself comments that

> . . . the first stanza approaches peace as *pax*, an understanding of peace based on a cessation of conflict. The second stanza offers a picture of a more dynamic view of peace as *shalom*, the condition of living abundantly

in harmony and mutual goodwill. Although the text affirms that peace is always God's gift, it also recognizes the importance of human responsibility in preparing an environment in which peace can flourish."[35]

❧

If you have ever been in an English congregation singing Parry's "Jerusalem" with its original text by the poet William Blake, you know what it means to say that your heart "swells."

> And did those feet in ancient time
> Walk upon England's mountains green?
> And was the Holy Lamb of God
> On England's pleasant pastures seen?
>
> And did the countenance divine
> Shine forth upon our clouded hills?
> And was Jerusalem builded here
> Among these dark satanic mills?
>
> Bring me my bow of burning gold!
> Bring me my arrows of desire!
> Bring me my spear! O clouds, unfold!
> Bring me my chariot of fire!
>
> I will not cease from mental fight,
> Nor shall my sword sleep in my hand,
> Till we have built Jerusalem
> In England's green and pleasant land.[36]

This beloved hymn is sung with zest—both in great gatherings for worship and smaller gatherings, such as the women's organization in England nicknamed "The Jam and Jerusalem Society," because they sing Parry's text at each meeting and support their charitable endeavors by making homemade jam. It is, almost, an alternative national anthem, much like "O Beautiful for Spacious Skies" for the United States citizen who wishes to sing with ardor about his native land.

My husband and I have commented that, despite the fact that we are not citizens of "England's green and pleasant land," our hearts swell too when we sing "Jerusalem." This is a tribute to the power of music, but also a tribute to the power of suggestion. Our hearts swell with a false nostalgia for the legend that Jesus might indeed have visited this island, or at least Joseph of Arimathea, who brought a piece of the thorn bush that still grows near the ruins Glastonbury Abbey. They swell with hope for the future of England, although we do not even live there!

So we are indebted to Carl P. Daw, Jr., who has given us an alternative text for this stirring tune. Singing his text instead of Blake's is like putting a wide angle lens on your camera in order to take a more expansive photograph. While before we were focusing on only a small green island, our new lens can help us see the entire planet.

Daw's strong text helps our ardent yearning expand as well. He directs this yearning toward the hope that the entire "warring world" can become Jerusalem, the city of peace, *shalom*, or *salem*. No weapons are needed for this transformation; we can dispose of Blake's bows and arrows, spears and chariots. Swords of hate fall from our hands as envy falls from our hearts. All creation will be included in this longed-for world of peace; the wolf will dwell with the lamb, the Arab with the Jew, the Serb with the Albanian, the Christian with the Muslim. "All creatures will find their true accord; / the hope of peace shall be fulfilled, / for all the earth shall know the Lord."

Last Sunday after Epiphany

Hymn 122,123   Alleluia, song of gladness
Latin, 11th cent.; tr. *John Mason Neale (1818–1866)**

"Alleluia, song of gladness" is based on a translation by Neale of the medieval hymn *Alleluia, dulce carmen*. Because the medieval church forbade the use of alleluias during Lent, some local rites included ceremonies of "bidding farewell" to Alleluias. In Toul in northeastern France, for example, the manuscript of *Alleluia, dulce carmen* was buried accompanied by the full ritual of a Requiem Mass.

The hymn readies the worshiper for an impending exile which is likened to the Babylonian captivity of the Jews, who sat down and wept "by the waters of Babylon." (Ps. 137) The forthcoming season of fasting will be a time of longing for Easter, when once again "alleluia" will resound with all the saints on high in the "true Jerusalem and free."

The text is matched with two chant tunes, the first in speech rhythm, the second a strong rhythmic arrangement which may be accompanied by handbells and percussion.

❧

Our liturgical year, along with the hymns that mark its seasons, reminds us that we are creatures both of time and of eternity. This is one of the many paradoxes which shape our lives as Christians.

We teach our children that "God is everywhere," yet take

---

*For additional biographical information, see *A Closer Walk*, 65–67.

them to worship in "God's house." In our prayer, we sometimes experience an eternal, transcendent God, and at other times feel the nearness of our personal Savior. And here we are, on the brink of Lent, bidding farewell to alleluias because we are about to walk the way of the historical Jesus right up to Golgotha, at the same time singing that alleluia is the "voice of joy that cannot die"!

The paradox of our faith is obvious during Lent, the penitential season of preparation for the most glorious of festivals. The church was particularly astute about the human psyche when it provided us with a season that offers us dual opportunities. Simultaneously, we acknowledge our contrition for sin and anticipate the joy of Easter. We dwell in the presence of the eternal God and at the same time walk beside the incarnate Christ in his Passion and Crucifixion.

If, the entire year long, we confined ourselves to singing of praise to the eternal Creator, might not faith begin to lose its vigor? We would perhaps be in the situation of our former neighbors who moved from the mild climate of California to the New York suburbs, because they were bored with "being comfortable all the time."

On the other hand, if we focused on the story of Jesus alone, might we not find ourselves so immersed in the first century that we could not recognize the eternal hand of God in our own day and our own lives?

C.S. Lewis, the lay theologian and author, puts it well, in his *Letters of Malcolm*:

> It is well to have specifically holy places, and things, and days, for without these focal points or reminders, the belief that all is holy and "big with God" will soon dwindle into a mere sentiment. But if these holy places,

things, and days cease to remind us, if they obliterate our awareness that all ground is holy and every bush (could we but perceive it) a Burning Bush, then the hallows begin to do harm. Hence both the necessity, and the perennial danger, of religion.[37]

On my color-coded church year calendar, the numbers are still green for the season of Epiphany. But three days from now, they will be purple. The altar guild will have been busy changing the hangings in the church, the anthems will be more somber, and, above all, we will have to forego "alleluias" until the Easter Vigil.

I need these reminders that I live in history, not just in eternity. I need seasons for introversion, like the one that will begin three days hence, when I cannot avoid looking within myself to discover the ways my behavior contributes to sorrow in the world.

But this season without "alleluias" is set within a larger context: the context of the next bright season, when the numbers on my calendar turn a blazing white. For in eternity, it is always Easter, and it is for eternity we are destined.

Ash Wednesday

Hymn 145   Now quit your care
Percy Dearmer (1867–1936)

Percy Dearmer was educated at Christ Church, Oxford. He was a priest, social activist, Red Cross chaplain, professor of ecclesiastical art, canon of Westminster, leader in the London Christian Social Union, and a prolific writer and hymnodist.

Dearmer was one of seven scholars of the "High Church Party" who decided to compile a hymnal that might become "a humble companion to the Book of Common Prayer."[38] The result was *The English Hymnal*, published in London in 1906. Its musical editors were Ralph Vaughan Williams and Martin Shaw, Dearmer's organist at St. Mary the Virgin, Primrose Hill. The book included texts by the English writers Heber, Keble, Christopher Wordsworth, Cowper, Doddridge, Watts, translations from Latin and Greek by John Mason Neale and from German by Catherine Winkworth and Robert Bridges, and American texts which included works by Whittier, Bryant, Holmes, Lowell, and George W. Doane.

In Isaiah 58:1–12, one of the Old Testament lessons appointed for the Ash Wednesday liturgy, the prophet declares to God's people that their fasting is unacceptable and that God prefers acts of justice and peace:

> Such fasting as you do today will not make your voice heard on high. . . . Is not this the fast that I choose: to loose the bonds of injustice, to undo the thongs of the yoke, to let the oppressed go free, and to break every yoke? Is it not to share your bread with the hungry and bring the homeless poor into your house; when you see the naked, to cover them, and not to hide yourself from your own kin?

Dearmer took these references in Isaiah, along with Jesus' injunction about fasting in the sixth chapter of the gospel according to Matthew ("Whenever you fast, do not look dismal, like the hypocrites") and the Beatitudes from the Sermon on the Mount to create his Lenten hymn.

The text was written for use with the French carol tune *Quittez, Pasteurs*, Dearmer used the French poem as a model for his own hymn. Although its Christmas pastoral setting is quite different from his own subject matter, the opening line echoes the *quittez* of the French and the poet follows the rhyme scheme of the original.

&

"Quit it!" my brothers and I would yell when sibling teasing got out of hand. Our lives can get out of hand, as well, and Lent is a chance to "quit it!"

Recently we met friends whom we haven't seen much of lately. "We're so busy, so tired, we just don't have a life," they complained. To outward appearances, and according to our cultural standards, they do indeed have a life: they have two homes, two cars, successful careers, plenty of money, and important roles in their community.

But they are burdened, bound, and imprisoned by too much to do in the finite number of hours in each day. Instead of just mumbling some sympathetic words, I suppose that I should have suggested that they read Percy Dearmer's text. For this season is a gift to our busy friends, and to everyone in similar predicaments.

Lent helps us notice our burdens, and to "quit" trying to carry all of them. Just as the word "burden" has evolved from meaning simply "something that is carried" to meaning "something oppressive or worrisome," so it can be with the activities and responsibilities of our lives. What might begin as a series of stimulating challenges, can, over time, become too much for us to carry.

Lent can be a time to take those burdens off our backs, to place them directly in front of us, and to decide what to do about them.

Some of these burdens are emotional: "care," "anxious

fear," "worry." As we move through this season in which we remember Jesus' love for us, we may finally realize that we do not need to carry this kind of burden alone; we can put our anxieties into the hands of God.

Some of the burdens we carry are caused by our desire to control events, although "schemes are vain / and fretting brings no gain." We can, through prayer and meditation, learn, in the words of the Beatles, to "let it be."

Or perhaps our burdens are those of unresolved guilt, a kind of "sackcloth and ashes" of the psyche. Lent is a good time to move from guilt into genuine repentance, confess the things that are bothering us, and discover that God's forgiveness is always there, waiting for us to accept it.

Lent helps us rediscover the true values we hold, so that we can adjust our lives accordingly. It is a time to celebrate our call to make a difference in the lives of others by setting wrongs to right, shattering every yoke, putting oppression to flight, and feeding the hungry.

These gospel directives are not another burden: instead, they are meant to help us, at the same time that we are helping others. If we are so caught up in the race towards success that we are unable to see the real needs in the world around us, we will not be living fully as human beings. The outcome of "quitting our care" is not only righteousness, but peace; it helps our lives become light as the dawn breaking forth in the morning, it unlocks the life-giving fountain of health, and it causes friendship to blossom. It gives us a life.

"And love shall be the prize. / Arise, arise, / arise! and make a paradise!"

The more I think about it, the more I wish that I had suggested that my weary friends meditate on this hymn. There is, fortunately, still time do to so, at any season!

First Sunday in Lent

Hymn 150   Forty days and forty nights
George Hunt Smyttan (1822–1870)

George Hunt Smyttan was born in Bombay, India, the son of
a doctor of the Bombay Medical Board. He was educated at
Corpus Christi College, Cambridge, and ordained in 1848.
He served for a year as curate of Ellingham, near Alnwick, and
then for nine years was rector of Hawksworth, Nottingham-
shire, resigning because of ill health in 1859. He died suddenly, friendless and penniless, while traveling abroad and
was buried in a pauper's grave in Frankfurt-am-Main.

Smyttan was the author of *Thoughts in Verse for the Afflicted* (1849), *Florum Sacra, in simple verse* (1854), *Mission Songs
and Ballads* (1860), and four hymns that appeared in *Lyra
Eucharistica* (1864).

"Forty days and forty nights" is one of three Lenten poems by Smyttan published in the *Penny Post VI* in March
1856; it was entitled "As sorrowful, yet always rejoicing." Its
original nine stanzas recall the trials of Jesus' temptation in
the wilderness.

In 1861, Francis Pott, a priest, scholar, and translator of
Latin and Syriac hymns, undertook a major alteration of the
text before including it in his *Hymns fitted to the Order of Common Prayer*. Among the stanzas he omitted were the following:

> And shall we in silken ease,
> Festal mirth, carousals high,
> All that can our senses please,
> Let our Lenten hours pass by?

Shall we not with thee retire,
Far from all the giddy throng,
Searching out the heart's desire,
Mourning sin the whole day long?[39]

It is Pott's version of Smyttan's text that forms the foundation for the hymn as it appears in *The Hymnal 1982*.

The German chorale tune chosen by Pott has been associated with the text since 1861.

❧

I find myself saddened by my discovery that this hymnwriter died "friendless and penniless." Was Smyttan a curmudgeon? Was he a severe man? Or was he merely an extreme introvert?

His focus on the temptation of Jesus in the wilderness makes me wonder about his own inner wilderness, which may have caused him to become bereft of friendship at life's end. I wonder if he experienced life as a perpetual struggle with an inner foe, the personification of evil he called "Satan," the name used also by Jesus and his contemporaries.

Smyttan definitely understood Lent as a time of training for combat with this foe. It was like the training of a wrestler, and Jesus was his model for victorious struggle.

In our time, the word "tempt" has lost much of its power. It usually means only "to entice," as in "I'm tempted to take a vacation" or "I'm tempted to order the chocolate cake."

Its biblical meaning had a different tone: temptation was not mere enticement, but a challenge. It gave the person tempted an opportunity to strengthen the moral and spiritual "muscles," and to prove themselves faithful. During his forty days in the hot Judean desert, Jesus was tested in this way. Because he had great power, his temptations were dramatic ones. He could have used his power to transform stones into bread in order to satisfy his hunger. He could have deserted his true mission for the sake of political power. He could have put God to an arbitrary test and staged a spectacular miracle. That it was a time of struggle is demonstrated by the fact that afterwards he told the story to his disciples, who passed on the narrative until it was eventually recorded in three of the Gospels.

This great struggle in the wilderness is not as far removed from our own experience of temptation as we might think. For the power of evil is most insistent, and most destructive, when it infiltrates those aspects of ourselves that are our greatest gifts and abilities. Most of us could recite examples. Perhaps we have known an earnest and devout priest who, in her effort to do her best for a parish, eventually became so concerned that others might try to undermine her vision that she became suspicious to the point of paranoia. Or maybe we have voted for a candidate for public office because the force of his personality convinced us that he would respond to the needs of the citizen; after being elected, that same forceful personality led him to adopt a rigid and tyrannical way of governing.

So we should not be surprised when there happens to be a similar struggle within ourselves. It is not our weaknesses that have the capacity to harm others and ourselves, but our strengths. Perhaps it comes down to one question: do we use our gifts and abilities for God's purposes, or for ours? It is my experience that this is our repeated challenge, to which we need to apply all our muscle: of intellect, intuition, heart, and faith.

I hope that Smyttan did not see such challenges as the enticements of Satan, or signs of his own weakness, and thus grow into a bitter old man. Instead, I think, they are the exercise provided by life, and by the grace of God. They are exercise for the soul, helping us to learn to focus on our true goals in the Christian life, and to realize that we do not go through temptations alone, but that our Savior is always at our side.

Second Sunday in Lent

Hymn 401   The God of Abraham praise
Thomas Olivers (1725–1799)

Many individuals have had a share in the history of this hymn, known as the *Yigdal*. The first was Moses Maimonides, the great Hebrew scholar born in Cordoba, Spain, in 1135. In 1148, he fled from Cordoba with his family to escape persecution by the Muslims; the family finally settled in Morocco around 1160. There, Maimonides studied medicine and wrote treatises on the Jewish calendar and on logic.

The family next lived for a while in Alexandria and in Cairo, during which time Maimonides' brother David, a dealer in precious stones, drowned in the Indian Ocean while on a business trip. Maimonides, whose life of study and writing had been supported by his brother, became a physician to support himself, and eventually was appointed physician to the ruler of Egypt.

He soon became famous; according to legend, Richard the Lionhearted once sought his services. Maimonides' two major works are the *Mishnah Torah*, compiled in 1180, and the *Guide*, written in 1190. The *Yigdal* is his summary, in thirteen articles of faith, of the essential articles of Judaism.

A metrical version of this creed has been attributed to Daniel ben Judah, a liturgical poet who lived in Rome in the middle of the fourteenth century. It has been ascribed also to Immanuel ben Solomon, known in Italian as Manoello Guideo, an early fourteenth-century scholar and poet. This version has long been printed in Hebrew prayer books, and it usually is sung antiphonally in synagogues by the cantor and the congregation at the conclusion of the service on the eve of Sabbath and at festivals.

Finally, a Wesleyan preacher from Wales, Thomas Olivers, heard the *Yigdal* sung by Meyer Lyon, otherwise known as *Leoni*, at the Great Synagogue, Duke's Place, London, and was inspired to write an English version. Olivers is reported to have said, "Look at this; I have rendered it from the Hebrew, giving it, as far as I could, a Christian character, and I have called on Leoni, the Jew, who has given me a synagogue melody to suit it; here is the tune, and it is to be called *Leoni*."[40]

Published in 1772, the hymn was headed "A Hymn to the God of Abraham: in Three Parts: adapted to a celebrated Air, sung by the Priest, Signior Leoni, &c., at the Jews' Synagogue, in London." It became so popular that, by 1799, it had appeared in thirty editions.

The tune is an adaptation of the melody to which the *Yigdal* was sung when Olivers heard it in London.

∽

Thomas Cahill's book *The Gifts of the Jews* is subtitled *How a Tribe of Desert Nomads Changed the Way Everyone Thinks and Feels*.[41] The story of Abraham, he suggests, marked the turning point between two world views.

In the ancient Sumerian civilization, life was understood as cyclical. The wheel of life turned like the high vault of heaven; the gods were as remote as the moon and the stars.

It was in such a setting that, a century or so after the beginning of the second millennium B.C.E., Avram, son of Terrah, heard a voice: "Go from your country and your kindred and your father's house to the land that I will show you. I will make of you a great nation, and I will bless you, and make your name great, so that you will be a blessing." (Gen. 12:1–2)

So, *wayyelekh Avram* ("Avram went"). Cahill states that these are

> . . . two of the boldest words in all literature. They signal a complete departure from everything that has gone before in the long evolution of culture and sensibility. Out of Sumer, civilized repository of the predictable, comes a man who does not know where he is going but goes forth into the unknown wilderness under the prompting of his god.[42]

Eventually, this Avram will be called Abraham, signifying his new status. His name will now mean "the ancestor is exalted," and God will enter into the covenant which is the sign of a new relationship between Abraham's people and their deity.

Avram went. Religion would be no longer what it had been for the Sumerians and other ancient cultures: "impersonal manipulation by means of ritual prescriptions."[43] Instead, in the land of Canaan, a new theology was born. It grew out of a peoples' face-to-face relationship with an inscrutable wilderness God, upon whom they learned they could depend. Human consciousness had been altered, as, for the first time, human beings grasped the fact that they lived in linear history.

It is this God that is praised by three major religions: Judaism, Islam, and Christianity. This is a God who is vast as the terrain through which Abraham and his convoy made their way. This is the great "I AM" who speaks to the humblest soul as well as the greatest Semitic chieftain, the God upon whose oath of covenant love we can depend.

Abraham's God is not one we can tame or manipulate. Praying to this desert deity does not always make us feel comfortable. This God may ask us "to go"— to go beyond our self-interest, our convenience, our fears, our preconceptions about life. Abraham's God helps us walk forward into history—our history. "Enthroned above," this God also walks beside us, through the vast and unknown spaces of the years ahead of each of us.

Third Sunday in Lent

Hymn 146,147   Now let us all with one accord
Att. *Gregory the Great (540–604)**

Although the anonymous Lenten hymn *Ex more docti mystico* is found in several tenth-century manuscripts, it may be much older. It has been attributed to Gregory the Great.

The paraphrase first appeared in the English Roman Catholic hymnal *Praise the Lord* in 1972, and the translator has been identified as James Quinn, S.J.**

The text is matched with a plainchant tune long associated with the text, as well as with a nineteenth-century rural American tune.

&

---

* For biographical information, see *A Closer Walk*, 71–73.
** For biographical information, see *Awake, My Soul!*, 204.

On a cold winter evening, I join a silent vigil, holding a candle in the dark along with two hundred others. A woman in our small town has been accused of producing pornography by a series of zealous people, from a clerk in a photo-developing lab to a county prosecutor. She is a good mother who serves the community well—particularly, and ironically, the children of the community. Her child's teacher, her friends, and her colleagues, have all testified to her innocence in responding to her daughter's request for a bathtime photo of herself, after a class trip to an art museum where the child had admired a photograph of a beautiful woman bathing.

The root of the word which describes what we are doing means "watchfulness," "keeping awake." The crowd includes all kinds of people, from professors and housewives to house painters, poets, and a priest. We are here because, at the moment, our friend and her family are suffering. We have already expressed our support through a political demonstration on the courthouse steps and through letters and phone calls to the county authorities. Now we need to express our support through this ritual of light and silence. We are here because, at the moment, her predicament has become the center of community concern. We are "watching over," her, in solidarity and sympathy.

We are also watching in another way. We are showing her accusers that we are awake to her innocence: we know that she is a good mother and a good citizen. The very process of watching awakens us and others to our responsibilities to safeguard our own freedoms and family privacy, at the same time we are awake to the societal and legal dilemmas about how to prevent child pornography.

What does this vigil on the town square have to do with the watch we keep during Lent? In Lent, we focus on Jesus in much the same way that our small town has focused on this woman and her family. We allow his presence to stand out from the crowd—the "crowd" of our busy and preoccupied lives. We hear the stories of his temptation in the wilderness and we awaken to our own vulnerability to evil. We follow his steps to Gethsemane and awaken to our own capacity for betrayal of God's image in ourselves and others. We follow him to Golgotha and awaken to the ultimate sign of covenant love: God's Son nailed to the cross.

Our vigil with Christ helps us to understand how important our other vigils are, from community vigils like the one for our friend to our more solitary vigils at a parent's deathbed.

Sometimes, when our meditation upon life draws us into mystery, words and action do not suffice. It is then that our truest response is to go beyond words to silence and beyond action to stillness, keeping vigil with our heavenly Lord—and also with our earthly neighbors.

Fourth Sunday in Lent

Hymn 693   Just as I am, without one plea
Charlotte Elliott (1789–1871)

Some of the most popular hymns of the Victorian era were "invalid hymns," and many of these were written by Charlotte Elliott. Elliott was born in Clapham, England. She began at an early age to write humorous poems, and was interested in music and painting. At the age of thirty-two, she suffered an illness which resulted in her becoming a permanent invalid. The next year, she met César Malan, an evangelist from

Geneva, who inspired her to devote the rest of her life to religious and humanitarian pursuits. Her correspondence with him lasted forty years.

In 1834 she undertook to edit the *Christian Remembrancer Pocketbook*, and prepared this volume annually for twenty-five years. She assisted in the publication of *The Invalid's Hymn Book*, printed in Dublin in 1836. Her hymns appear in that collection, as well as in many others: *Hours of Sorrow Cheered and Comforted* (1836); *Hymns for a Week* (1839); *Thoughts in Verse on Sacred Subjects* (1869); and her brother's collection *Psalms and Hymns for Public, Private, and Social Worship* (1838–1848).

This hymn first appeared in Elliott's *Invalid's Hymn Book* with the heading, "Him that cometh unto Me, I will in no wise cast out" (Jn.6:37). It was written at Westfield Lodge, Brighton, where her brother, the Rev. Henry V. Elliott, had arranged a bazaar to raise funds for building a college, to be named St. Margaret's Hall. Because she was neither able to attend or to help in any way, Elliott, oppressed by feelings of uselessness, finally penned the poem in order to overcome her sense of futility. The irony of the story is that the sale of this hymn aided the cause more than any bazaar: the title page of the various editions of *Hymns for a Week*, in which it was later published, contain the note, "Sold for the benefit of St. Margaret's Hall, Brighton."

The hymn was a great favorite of William Wordsworth's daughter, Dora, whose widower sent a message to Elliott in July of 1847 to thank her for her beautiful hymn. It had been of great comfort to his wife while she lay on her death bed: "I do not think Mr. Wordsworth could bear to have it repeated in his presence, but he is not the less sensible of the solace it gave his one and matchless daughter."[44]

A similar tribute was given by Elliott's brother, who wrote, "In the course of a long ministry, I hope I have been permitted to see some fruit of my labors; but I feel far more has been done by a single hymn of my sister's."[45] After her death, more than a thousand letters were found among her belongings thanking her for the hymn.

The text is matched with the tune with which it has been popularly associated in the United States since 1860.

&

I used to smile at what I considered to be the sentimentality of this hymn text until I read the story of Charlotte Elliott. An invalid who ministered to others through her poetry, she obviously met a real need in an era before awareness of preventive health care and the miracles of modern medicine were the norm. Her *Hours of Sorrow Cheered and Comforted* contained titles such as: "On a restless night in illness," "To one whose mind was disordered by grief," "To a mother, on the death of a child of great promise," and "To one deprived of hearing at church through deafness." Because she herself had studied in the school of suffering, she could teach others. She spoke to people who felt useless or stricken, and her words rang true.

It is only to healthy people in the prime of life in the twenty-first century that these words are likely to sound sentimental. There are many others who have learned, through hard experience, the wisdom of Elliott's words.

I frequently visit a local extended care retirement community where there is a nursing wing. Residents of the independent living units who are ill or have undergone surgery may stay in the nursing wing for a time until they have strength to manage life on their own. But there are some permanent residents of the nursing wing who could tell us a great deal about uselessness.

Some of them could have written a poem similar to Elliott's. There is a beautiful woman who owned a fashionable dress shop on the East Coast until a stroke deprived her of speech. No longer an efficient and successful businesswoman, she is nevertheless a smiling presence in the retirement center, cheering others by her wonderful outfits and flamboyant earrings and her obvious zest for life.

Her neighbor is a widow with what is called "brittle" diabetes, and her insulin level must be monitored day and night. We had looked at the gracious and hospitable house she had lived in when we were seeking a place to live in Oberlin, and I was drawn to her warmth and friendliness. These qualities have not diminished since she became a resident in the nursing wing; she herself embodies the hospitality I recognized in her former home.

There is a young man named Jeff who is afflicted with Lou Gehrig's Disease, or Amyotrophic Lateral Sclerosis, a progressive degeneration of the nerve cells in the brain and spinal cord that control the voluntary muscles. The illness, mercifully, does not at this point affect his mind, but Jeff cannot move and he spends his waking hours in a wheel chair. His call button for the nursing station is a mouth-operated device. He cannot feed himself, but depends on the resident assistants and the good will of volunteers from the retirement community.

When I asked Jeff how he was the other day, he said, "I'm fine; I'm just 'Jeffing.'" He could have said, "Just as I am without one plea." Jeff has learned a new approach to life, in which the value of thoughtful, reflective being supersedes the usual societal value given to usefulness. Because he is so good at "Jeffing," Jeff has many visitors: professors, students, retirement community residents, people from the town, and myself. Going to see Jeff is like visiting a guru, who reminds us of why we are called human *beings*, rather than human *doings*.

I would like to think that we can all learn the value of "Jeffing" or "Nancying" or "Whatever-your-name-is-ing" without being struck by illness or accident or extreme old age. Our whole lives long, we need to remind ourselves that we are valuable in God's eyes, not because we are capable, but because we are ourselves.

I am sure that none of us arrives at that insight easily. It is human nature to resist dependence and weakness with all our power: very likely we would be "tossed about / with many a conflict, many a doubt," should we ourselves end up in a wheelchair. Elliott's poem reassures us that, on the other side of that struggle, lies a treasure: the absolute dependence, not merely on others, but on the fact that God's great love, with all its breadth, length, depth, and height, is ours, just as we are.

Fifth Sunday in Lent

Hymn 170   To mock your reign, O dearest Lord
*F. Pratt Green (b. 1903)**

In 1972, F. Pratt Green received a letter from the British composer Francis Westbrook:

> I am haunted by the almost unearthly beauty of Tallis'
> THIRD MODE MELODY. You will know it. It is set to
> some impossible words by Addison in the *English*

---

*For additional biographical information, see *Awake, My Soul!*, 159–160.

Hymnal. . . . Can you try your hand at three verses? I
want to write an anthem on the tune. It seems to call
for something virile yet wistful.[46]

The resulting text by Green graphically describes the
scourging of Jesus recounted in Matthew 27:30. Green's
poem is in the tradition of the Metaphysical poets, under-
scoring the paradox of the events of Good Friday through
strong imagery: the Passion of Christ is "a soldier's joke," yet
the crown of thorns will flower upon Christ's brow.

❧

You never can be sure about a person's real identity.

I once knew a woman from an aristocratic English family
who had also been given a title of her own. Like many of
noble birth, she marched to her own drummer and took little
notice of her appearance. One day, when her travels took her
to New York, we agreed to meet in Grand Central Station
and go to dinner together. It was in the era when the station
was still a shelter for the many homeless of the city. My heart
sank when I saw her. She was, to put it diplomatically, bedraggled. Would they let us in the restaurant? I understood
the power of the clerical collar when they welcomed us and
led us to a table for two. When she died a few years ago, her
funeral rites, held in a great English cathedral, were attended
by hundreds.

A well-known ballerina lived in our town for a while.
Perhaps to counteract her brilliant stage image, she chose to
dress like a ragamuffin, fastening her clothing with safety
pins, which became her fashion trademark. She certainly
stood out on the train platform among the commuters
dressed for success. She, unlike most of them, however, will
have a place in the history books.

A black youth in our suburban community, the son of a prominent doctor, was often stopped and questioned by the police as he walked home from high school, not because of his clothing but simply because of the color of his skin—a scenario played and replayed in our society.

It makes me think about how easy it would have been to jump to conclusions about the bedraggled, bloodied man taunted by Roman soldiers on Good Friday. We can express our horror at the grim charade, but we have the benefit of history. We, who have read the Gospels, think that we would not make the mistake the soldiers made. Certainly, *we* would have recognized Jesus for who he was.

But would we have recognized him if we had known nothing about him? We may not have had the soldiers' capacity for cruelty, but we might well have passed by quickly, averting our eyes like city-dwellers hurrying by a homeless woman huddled for warmth on a sidewalk grate.

A friend who is a prominent churchman recently shared the story of his son, who lived "on the streets" for several years, lost to his family despite all their efforts to help. He said that, every time they saw a homeless man, they looked carefully: "Each one might have been our son."

You can never be sure about the stranger. The safest policy is to treat all whom you encounter with respect and kindness. She might be a noblewoman or a ballerina. He might be a doctor's son or your own son. Or, even, your Lord.

The Sunday of the Passion: Palm Sunday

Hymn 154,155   All glory, laud, and honor
Theodulph of Orleans (d. 821); tr. *John Mason Neale (1818–1866)*

Theodulph was born in Spain, around 750, and named Bishop of Orleans by the Emperor Charlemagne in 781. He remained an influential theologian and counselor to the emperor throughout his reign. During the period of political intrigue following the emperor's death, Theodulph was accused of complicity in a plot to overthrow King Louis I. Although he heartily denied the accusation, he was removed from his see and imprisoned at Angers.

In his *Elucidatorium ecclesiasticum* (1516), Josse Clichtove tells of a happy outcome for Theodulph:

> On Palm Sunday, 821, Louis the Pious, King of France, was at Angers and took part in the usual procession of the clergy and laity. As the procession passed the place where St. Theodulph was incarcerated he stood at the open window of his cell, and amid the silence of the people, sung this hymn which he had newly composed. The king was so much delighted with the hymn that he at once ordered St. Theodolph to be set at liberty and restored to his see; and ordained that henceforth, the hymn should always be used in processions on Palm Sunday.[47]

Sadly, this is an apocryphal story, perhaps the product of wishful thinking, for Theodulph remained a prisoner until his death, possibly of poisoning, that same year.

Since medieval times, *Gloria, laus et honor* has been used as a processional on Palm Sunday. The text is set either to a strong German choral tune or to its historic chant tune in a rhythmic setting.

❧

The drama of Palm Sunday is similar to what it must feel like to hike through a beautiful mountain meadow enjoying the scenery and suddenly stumble and plunge into a dark abyss. The liturgy begins in exaltation: the acclamation "Blessed is the King who comes in the name of the Lord: Peace in heaven and glory in the highest."[48] We soon hear the story which is the setting of that acclamation. As Jesus draws near to Jerusalem, the disciples find a colt and Jesus is set upon it. The excited multitudes spread their garments on the road like a royal carpet, strew the way with palms, and cry out their enthusiastic greeting.

In our churches today, after the blessing of the palms, worshipers reenact this story of the triumphal entry, clasping palm branches during the liturgical procession, which some-times takes us outdoors on a sunny springtime Sunday, while we sing this triumphant hymn.

This procession is one of my most vivid childhood memories of church, possibly because children love parades. I know that when I act out the story with very young children, they can never get enough of the triumphal entry. I used to have a collection of our sons' outgrown t-shirts, which were a useful prop for spreading on the portion of the Sunday school room which served as the road to Jerusalem. What was remarkable was the role most of the children chose to take. Not a member of the palm-waving crowd; not even Jesus. Most of them wanted to be the colt, or the "donkey." So our enactments were anomalies, with many donkeys, a small crowd, and only an imaginary Jesus.

I've often wondered why that happened. Was it the children's natural affinity for animals, or the fact that they knew intuitively that carrying Jesus would have been, indeed, an important role.

I think about the "triumphal entry" times in my own life, when it felt as if I were at the peak of usefulness in ministry, "carrying Jesus" to others in ways that were exciting and exhilarating. Sometimes, at the end of that path, lay a metaphorical Jerusalem. The rest of the Palm Sunday liturgy reminds us of what happened in Jerusalem at the end of Jesus' exultant parade: conflict, betrayal, loss, struggle, betrayal, and death.

Our own Jerusalems may not be as dramatic, but they remind us that we can never take for granted the times when we are feeling acclaimed and supported. We may stumble into the abyss at any moment, and find that the voices calling to us are no longer welcoming ones.

At those times, we learn that the children who chose to be the colt, in their innocence, knew only half the truth. Sometimes we need to stop trying to carry Jesus, and reverse the roles. For the way to carry Jesus, and his message of love and compassion, during our own Jerusalems is to let Jesus—his story, his self-giving love, his presence—carry us.

Monday in Holy Week

Hymn 642   Jesus, the very thought of thee
Latin, 12th cent.; st. 5, *Latin, 15th cent.*; tr. *Edward Caswall*
(1814–1878)

The hymn *Jesu dulcis memoria* (or *Dulcis Jesu memoria*) has often been attributed to Bernard of Clairvaux, but more recent scholarship supports the view that it is from the pen of an unknown author of the twelfth century. The intensely personal devotion of the poem is, however, in keeping with Bernard's spirit.

The original Latin poem has forty-two stanzas. It is possible that the author was English, as the earliest and best manuscripts are from England.

Most early manuscripts do not indicate a particular use for the poem, although several label it a devotion on the name of Jesus, and one thirteenth-century missal places it among prayers of preparation for communion. Eventually the text became ssociated with the Feast of the Name of Jesus, which was first observed around 1500.

Because of its length, subjectivity, and the use of the first person throughout, it is likely that the poem was intended for private devotional use, rather than for a liturgical context.

In David Livingston's diary, the following entry is found referring to *Jesu dulcis memoria*: "That hymn of St. Bernard, on the name of Christ, although in what might be termed dog-Latin, pleases me so; it rings in my ears as I wander across the wide, wide wilderness."[49]

The translator Edward Caswall was an Anglican priest born

in Hampshire and educated at Oxford. He became a Roman Catholic in 1847. After he became a widower, he entered Newman's Oratory of St. Philip Neri, where he remained until his death. He wrote several devotional works and sacred poems, as well as translations of medieval Latin hymns, many of which were published in *Lyra Catholica* in 1857.

The text is matched with a sixteenth-century psalm tune of particular poignancy.

❧

In his fascinating book *Hymns and the Christian Myth*, Lionel Adey comments that *Dulcis Jesu memoria* conveys "a supreme insight that may well outlast the images of Christ as Victor, King, and even Victim: Jesus as the true source and object of what C.S. Lewis called *Sehnsucht*, literally a 'yearning,' appeasable only by his presence."[50]

Devotion to this Jesus—the object of our yearning and the fulfillment of our desires—has been the source of much great religious art, poetry, and music. My favorite examples are two duets in Johann Sebastian Bach's Cantata 140. A soprano and a bass represent the soul and Jesus as they sing, "When com'st Thou, my Lord?" "Beloved, I come." Later, they will sing "My love is thine! Our love shall stand forever. I follow thee to feed among the lilies, where fullness of joy is, and rest evermore."[51] These are tender love songs with sacred words, embedded in Bach's splendid cantata *Wachet auf, ruft uns die Stimme*, based on the parable of the wise and foolish virgins awaiting the bridegroom.

Like Bach's ardent duets, the twelfth-century Latin text *Jesu dulcis memoria* awakens my heart to the sustaining power of devotion to the second person of the Trinity. No wonder that this hymn rang in the ears of David Livingston as he wandered across the African wilderness. His love of Jesus not only provided the solace of Jesus' presence and protection; it generated energy and courage and provided an eternal goal beyond Livingston's earthly explorations.

It is not surprising that the "Jesus Prayer" has been much prayed by Christians, especially by Eastern Orthodox Christians, for almost two millennia. This prayer is the simple repetition of "Lord Jesus Christ, Son of God, have mercy on me, a sinner"—or one of its many abbreviated versions, such as "Jesus, mercy" or simply "Jesus." Eventually it becomes as habitual as the breath, continuing in the unconscious even when the conscious mind is occupied with other things. But it begins with yearning: for Jesus, for mercy, for understanding, for the presence of the one who, alone, can satisfy our hunger for love.

Tuesday in Holy Week

Hymn 167   There is a green hill far away
*Cecil Frances Alexander (1818–1895)**

This is one of a series of Cecil Frances Alexander's hymns for children based on the articles of the Apostles' Creed (see "Once in royal David's city," Christmas Day III). It forms a commentary on the fourth article, "Suffered under Pontius Pilate, was crucified, dead, and buried." The picture of the "green hill far away, outside a city wall," according to Percy Dearmer, has its genesis in the Irish landscape. "When she went shopping in Derry she had to drive by a little grassy hill

---

*For additional biographical background, see *A Closer Walk*, 46–47.

near the road, and she tells us that she used to fancy this was like Calvary."[52]

Her understanding of the Crucifixion harks back to Anselm, Archbishop of Canterbury between 1093 and 1109, who taught that amends for humanity's sinfulness could only be made to God by Jesus who was both God and man. The reward for this sacrifice of himself on the cross was our redemption. In the words of Albert Bailey, "More recent theories of the Atonement make all these ideas unacceptable to many: at any rate they are beyond the comprehension of children. While, therefore, its poetic fervor and the appealing tune (Green Hill), to which it is almost universally set, have made the hymn a great favorite with adults, one can only regret that it perpetuates an outworn theology."[53]

&

When I first went to Sunday school at the age of five, I learned "There is a green hill far away" in its *Hymnal 1940* version, in which the next words are "without a city wall." I felt sorry for that hill which lacked a city wall, although I did not understand why a hill would have a city wall in the first place. The hills I knew did not. I supposed I finally resigned myself to the fact that Jesus lived long ago in a faraway place where things were different.

I was puzzled by the hill without a wall, but I understood the final stanza: "O dearly, dearly, has he loved! / And we must love him too." I was not concerned about theological theories; all I knew was that Jesus had done this thing on my behalf. And I knew he "died to make [me] good."

According to the hymnologist Lionel Adey, I responded just as Mrs. Alexander would have hoped:

Mrs. Alexander dwells not on the suffering but on its redemptive purpose. She presents Christ as archetype of virtue, alone "good enough" to unlock Heaven's gate. Her hymn demands the responses of love, trust, and imitation, not of Christ's death, but of his "work". . . . Sparing infant sensibilities . . . she represents the Crucifixion at a great distance. This her finest hymn cultivates the feelings of children about the idea, rather than the mental image, of the suffering Christ. It invites children to feel and resolve, rather than behold and worship.[54]

It was amazing to me that someone would actually *die* for me. But this hymn said that Jesus had done just that, and that because of what happened on the green hill far away, I would someday go to heaven, especially if I tried with all my might to be good.

It may be that learning this hymn marked the beginning of my conscious struggle with sin, which at that time I interpreted as getting into fights with my sometimes irritating little brother or not always minding my mother as quickly or as willingly as God would have wanted.

My resolve to be good did not spring from fear of God's punishment, for, despite the theology embedded in this text, the tone of the hymn is that of love. I tried to be good because Jesus loved me, and I, in turn, loved him.

The struggle with sin has become far more complex with each passing year, but I like to think that the seeds of my desire to become a person of goodness were sown long ago, when I first sang about the dear Lord who died to save us all.

Wednesday in Holy Week

Hymn 337   And now, O Father, mindful of the love
William Bright (1824–1901)

William Bright was born in Doncaster, England, and educated at Rugby and University College, Oxford, where he was a theological scholar and won the Ellerton Theological Essay Prize. He was ordained in 1848 and served as a tutor at Trinity College, Glenalmond, before returning to Oxford as Regius Professor of Ecclesiastical History. In 1859, he was named canon of Christ Church. He was a prodigious scholar and prolific writer. Among his works are a number of books on early church history and poetry, including *Athanasius and other Poems* and *Hymns and Other Poems*. Many of the collects in the 1928 revision of the Book of Common Prayer were taken from Bright's *Ancient Collects and Other Prayers, selected for devotional use from various Rituals*. Some authorities have claimed that, when it came to writing collects, he was Cranmer's equal.

This hymn is a paraphrase of the oblation from the canon of the Latin Mass, *Unde et memores, Domini, nos servitui* ("and now, mindful of the Lord, your servants . . .") It was first published in *The Monthly Packet* in 1873 and was included in the 1875 edition of *Hymns Ancient and Modern*. The English preacher and social reformer H. Scott Holland wrote, "It is worth living to have left behind one such hymn which will be sung by unnumbered generations."[55]

The text is matched with a tune composed for it by one of Bright's contemporaries.   ♋

This hymn is proof to me of how often music can sweep me along so that I do not really notice what I am singing. When I look carefully at William Bright's text, I find that I have some problems with the theology that is assumed by the poet, although he is not alone in holding this view of the meaning of the Crucifixion.

Different views of the Crucifixion's meaning are called "theologies of the Atonement." "Atonement" can be understood by simply separating the word into three parts: at—one—ment. For centuries, theologians have asked, "How did Jesus' death on the Cross bring humanity into unity with the God from whom we were separated?"

In the hymns we sing during Lent, many views are represented. For example, the Latin hymn "Sing, my tongue, the glorious battle" (Hymns 165, 166) celebrates the Crucifixion as Jesus' victory over evil. Many centuries later, the poet Crossman understood Good Friday as Jesus' demonstration of unconditional and self-sacrificing love for us, as we learn when we sing his text "My song is love unknown" (Hymn 458).

In Bright's hymn, Jesus is seen as a sacrifice offered to the Father as a propitiation for our sins. The Crucifixion was, in the words of the Eucharistic Prayer of Rite I, an act "by his one oblation of himself once offered, a full, perfect, and sufficient sacrifice, oblation, and satisfaction, for the sins of the whole world."[56]

I struggle to understand this view, which is held by many Christians. Does it imply a difference of opinion between the Father and the Son? Does the Father want to judge and punish us, and is prevented from doing so because Jesus stands "between our sins and their reward"? Did Jesus somehow "buy" us from our own Creator, by paying the debt for our sins?

The best I can do is to work with the word "sacrifice," which has at its root two words: *sacer*, which means "holy" and *facere*, which means "to make." Perhaps Jesus is a sacrifice not because he is an offering *instead* of us, but because his self-offering on the Cross literally *makes holy* this fragile and failed humanity of ours. Perhaps, through him, we are given the capacity for holiness and for at-one-ment with our God.

I do not know the whole truth; no one can, in this life. As with all the things of God, the Atonement is, at its foundation, a mystery.

Perhaps, since I cannot fathom the Atonement, I should, as this hymn reminds me, be content to be mindful of the love represented by Calvary. That love frees me from theory and teaches me practice. It reminds me that, through Jesus' example, we discover that it is possible to make all things holy: the bread and the wine of the Eucharist, as well as every moment of the days God has given us.

Maundy Thursday

Hymn 322   When Jesus died to save us
St. 1, *F. Bland Tucker (1895–1984)*; st. 2, att. *John Donne (1573–1631)*

The second quatrain of this poem has sometimes been attributed either to the poet John Donne or to Queen Elizabeth I, who could have written it during the time she was imprisoned in the Tower of London by Queen Mary. However, it may well have been written during an earlier period. The clue is that the implicit questions being answered by the statements are reminiscent of a period between 1549 and 1559, when the revisions of the Book of Common Prayer sparked controversies about the Eucharist. There were differences of opinion about how Jesus' presence in the Eucharist was to be understood, which would have an impact upon the words to be used during the administration of communion.

In the 1549 Book of Common Prayer, there was a strong doctrine of the Real Presence. When distributing communion, the priest's words were the following: "The body [blood] of our Lord Jesus Christ which was given [shed] for thee, preserve thy body and soul unto everlasting life."

In the 1552 revision, the emphasis was not on the bread and the wine, but on the action of taking part in this sacrament as a remembrance of Jesus. The 1549 words of administration were replaced by "Take and eat this, in remembrance that Christ died for thee, and feed on him in thy heart by faith, with thanksgiving" and "Drink this in remembrance that Christ's blood was shed for thee, and be thankful."

Ultimately, in the 1559 Book of Common Prayer, the church chose a classic Anglican compromise, instructing the ministers of communion to say both the 1549 and the 1552 versions, joining them with an "and." (This remains one of the options in the Book of Common Prayer of the Episcopal Church for Holy Eucharist I, 338.)

The phrases in the second stanza of the hymn reflect a similar inclusive Anglican spirit. Through an allusion to John 1 ("In the beginning was the Word"), there is a reference to Jesus' words of institution at the Last Supper without the need to decide among the various gospel accounts. The final two lines are equally non-committal, declaring belief in Jesus' intention without specifying what that intention might have been ("what that Word did make it, / I do believe and take it").

The first stanza was written by F. Bland Tucker as an introduction to the original quatrain. Tucker admired the sixteenth-century poem as "a fine definition of Anglican theology, which holds to the fact but refuses to define too closely the mode."[57] Tucker's lines, in using "us" instead of "me," emphasize the corporate nature of the Eucharist and prepare the way for the individual's response in the second stanza.

The music was composed for use with this text by David Hurd, a contemporary American composer.

☙

I often think that young children are the ones who can best understand the Eucharist. Long before they are capable of abstract thought, they live easily in the world of symbols. They learn about the world through their experience of it, not through cogitation.

There is a transparency in their pleasure about being offered food. I love placing a wafer or piece of bread in a child's small hands at the altar rail. Often the response is "thank you," although one small child once tasted the homemade bread we use now in our parish and replied with a hearty "Yum!"—a reaction which would have delighted our Lord, this meal's true host, for whom meals were obviously a pleasure.

Once a small child came up clutching a teddy bear. After I placed a wafer in his free hand, he carefully "fed" some to his furry companion before he consumed it himself. He understood that this was a meal to be shared.

Children might write the second stanza of this hymn text in simpler language—something like "Jesus said this meal was for us, so it is a special meal and I am happy to eat it and share it." They do not get tied up in intellectual knots about why it is special, or who should share it.

On the other hand, it is in the nature of adult minds to try to figure things out. Why is this meal so special? How does it remind us of Jesus? What did Jesus mean when he said, "This is my body; this is my blood"?

It is all well and good to think about these things, but ultimately we come face to face with mystery. The fact is that, no matter how many theories we argue about with one another, all we can say for sure, in the end, is "He was the Word that spake it, / he took the bread and brake it, / and what that Word did make it, / I do believe and take it."

And we have been doing just that, through two thousand years of controversy about what that really means.

Good Friday

Hymn 441,442   In the cross of Christ I glory
John Bowring (1792–1872)*

The text of "In the cross of Christ I glory" was inspired by Galatians 6:14: "May I never boast of anything except the cross of our Lord Jesus Christ, by which the world has been crucified to me, and I to the world." It is obvious that Bowring, who was a Unitarian, was an unusual one, finding in Christ "all we know of God."[58]

The hymn was written in 1825, but years afterwards, when Bowring was governor of Hong Kong, he would see the cross which some believe inspired the text:

---

*For additional biographical background, see *Awake, My Soul!*, 15–17.

The first thing you see as you approach Macao (Island near Hong Kong) is the great white church of Our Lady of Fatima, perched on the island's highest hill. In a revolution the church was destroyed, save for the great west front. This west wall still stands and crowning the topmost point is a great metal cross, which (in repeated attacks) has survived destruction. It was this cross, blackened with smoke, that inspired John Bowring's hymn.[59]

Lionel Adey remarks that Bowring understood this symbol "towering over the wrecks of time" as a comfort rather than as a challenge to his life. In times of "woe and disappointment" it "glows with peace and joy," while in happier times its "radiance" adds luster to his "sun of bliss." That is why Bowring's Cross bears no figure.[60]

The opening line of the hymn was inscribed on Bowring's tombstone after his death in 1872.

The text was published in the collection *Hymns: as a Sequel to Matins*, in 1825 in London. The first tune provided was composed for use with the text by an American organist; the second is by a contemporary American composer.

℘

Paul's Epistle to the Galatians is a testament of Christian freedom. It grew out of controversy. Some teachers who had infiltrated the churches of Galatia declared that, in addition to having faith in Jesus Christ, a Christian was obligated to keep the law of Moses, which included the requirement of circumcision.

"No," said Paul. Before Jesus Christ came, the law was a necessary disciplinarian. "But now that faith has come, we are no longer subject to a disciplinarian, for in Christ Jesus you are all children of God through faith." (Gal.3:25–26) We do not any longer need to boast of our adherence to the law. "May I never boast of anything except the cross of our Lord Jesus Christ, by which the world has been crucified to me, and I to the world." (Gal.6:14)

For Paul, boasting of the cross of his Lord meant that he did not need to earn God's favor through his obedience to the law of Moses.

What does Bowring mean when he translates Paul's advice to the Galatians into "In the cross of Christ I glory"?

There are, in the *Oxford English Dictionary*, several meanings of the verb "glory": "to exult with triumph, to rejoice proudly"; "to boast"; "to give glory to, to honour." There is another use in the dictionary, when the verb is intransitive. It applies to light, and means "to spread like a glory," as in a halo.[61]

Bowring conflates these meanings; he boasts, rejoices in, and honors the cross of Christ, from which streams a radiance like a halo. His hymn is deeply personal, which is a good thing, because the cross, incorrectly understood, is itself responsible for an imperial view of Christianity which actually caused some of the "wrecks of time," including the bloodshed of the Crusades and the fanaticism of the Inquisition. In the imperial view, the cross, originally the means of a degrading death, can become a battering ram rather than a source of light.

For Bowring, however, the cross towers not over the earth and its institutions but over his life which, however successful outwardly, had its share of woes. Unlike the transient glory of parliamentary politics, the glamor of diplomatic life, and the renown of royal recognition, the glorious light of the cross was constant and eternal. When he and his wife were poisoned by opponents of his Hong Kong regime, the shadow of the cross reminded Bowring of the promise of everlasting life for his wife, and of healing for him.

The cross also shone upon his times of contentment and success, perhaps particularly during those hours when he was happily distant from a turbulent world, shut in his study writing his numerous translations, poems, and essays.

Although he does not mention it in his hymn, one suspects that the cross was not merely a comfort for Bowring, but had been, at least in the beginning of his life, a challenge, inspiring him during his early activist years to champion the downtrodden and oppressed.

Bowring's vision of the cross, embodied in this very personal hymn, is much like the small wooden crosses that some people carry in their pockets as a touchstone, or the silver or gold crosses hanging around their necks. For him as for St. Paul, it is a symbol of the sacred story: that Christ, crucified and risen, is still with us, in both sunshine and shadow.

Easter Vigil

Hymn 207   Jesus Christ is risen today
Latin, 14th cent.; tr. *Lyra Davidica, 1708*; St. 4, *Charles Wesley (1707–1788)*

"Jesus Christ is risen today" is based on the nine-stanza hymn *Surrexit Christus hodie*, which was found in three fourteenth-century manuscripts from Prague, Engleberg, and Munich.

The Latin hymn is a trope on the *Benedicamus Domino*,

which was sung at the end either of the Easter Mass or the Easter offices. "Troping"—making additions to the authorized text and music of the liturgy—was popular during the Middle Ages. The practice expanded to such an extent that the Council of Trent (1545–1563) ultimately abolished all embellishments to the liturgy with the exception of five authorized sequences.

A three-stanza English translation first appeared in *Lyra Davidica, or a Collection of Divine Songs and Hymns, partly New Composed, partly Translated from the High German and Latin Hymns: and set to easy and pleasant tunes, for more General Use*, published in London by a famous music printer, John Walsh in 1708. The fourth stanza, a doxology written by Charles Wesley, was added in 1862.

The melody for the text made its first appearance in *Lyra Davidica*, where the anonymous author made the comment that the purpose of the tunes in the book was to provide "a little freer air than the grave movement of the Psalm-tunes."[62]

☙

We once lived a few miles from a Russian Orthodox seminary, so that for several years I was able to celebrate Easter twice. The first one was at my suburban parish church at mid-morning on Easter Day. The familiar Easter hymns, the chorales and fanfares by visiting brass players, the special choir anthems, the Easter finery, the familiar faces, and the insistence of the preacher that the congregation shout "The Lord is risen indeed! Alleluia" when he proclaimed "Alleluia. Christ is risen!"—all spelled "Easter the way I have always known it."

My second Easter celebration usually occurred a week later at the Russian Orthodox Seminary, thanks to the discrepancy between the Eastern and Western liturgical calendars. On the Orthodox Easter Even, I stood in the midst of the congregation of St. Vladimir's, holding candles in the icon-lined seminary chapel. I knew very few people in the congregation, most of whom had broad Slavic faces.

The celebration lasted virtually the whole night long, beginning with the Easter offices. Immediately before the reading of the gospel, the chapel emptied, the door was shut, and a candlelit procession wove through the seminary garden. Back at the chapel door, the deacon read the gospel, the crucifer struck the door with his cross, and we gained entry in order to join the foretaste of the celestial banquet, mirrored here on earth so elaborately in this chapel on Easter Even. The general shape of the liturgy matched that in my Episcopal parish church, but the atmosphere had an exoticism and mystery that made these some of the most memorable Easter celebrations of my life. I can still hear the crowded chapel reverberating repeatedly with the Easter proclamation—"The Lord is risen! Indeed he has risen!" in English, Russian, and Greek, and without any prompting from the clergy. Morning was beginning to dawn when I made my way home, weary and exhilarated.

Since those days, I have had a few occasions to celebrate the Easter Vigil at a monastery or convent. After a few hours sleep, we rose while it was still dark, so that the igniting of the new fire was literally the first light. As the lessons were read, the sky began to lighten, until finally, at daybreak, the Eucharist began, and we were fed with the food of the Risen Lord.

These liturgies, it must be admitted, can be exhausting—perhaps, most of all, those at St. Vladimir's, where there were no pews or chairs. But the long nights of prayer and readings prepared us for a daybreak that was more than just the rising of the sun in the East. It was the blindingly joyous light of the rising of the Son.

"Jesus Christ is risen today!" "Alleluia! Christ is risen. The Lord is risen indeed. Alleluia!"

Easter Day

Hymn 183   Christians, to the Paschal victim
Wigbert (Wipo of Burgundy) (d.1050?); tr. The Antiphoner and Grail, 1880.

Both the text and tune of this Latin sequence were included in an eleventh-century manuscript from Einsiedeln, where it was ascribed to Wipo. Wipo was a Burgundian who served the German emperors Konrad II and his son, Heinrich III; during his time at the court, he recorded their lives and also presented collections of his poems to them.

Victimae Paschali Laudes is the oldest of the five sequences retained after the Council of Trent.* The hymn was used liturgically as a sequence both during the Mass on Easter and also during the following week.

The hymn was also the springboard from which liturgical drama came into being. The hymnologist Ryden describes the scene:

> This became a striking drama in which altar boys took the part of the two angels and three deacons represented the three Marys. In the dialogue which followed,

---

*See *Awake, My Soul!*, 112–113.

the angels asked, "Whom seek ye?" to which the Marys replied, "Jesus of Nazareth." The angels thereupon removed the white altar-cloth representing the grave clothes, and answered, "He is not here." The Marys then turned toward the choir and sang, "Alleluia, the Lord is risen." At this point the officiating bishop or succentor entered the liturgical drama by asking questions, to which the Marys replied by singing in turn various stanzas of *Victimae paschali*, in which the entire choir finally joined. At the conclusion of the rite, the bishop intoned the *Te Deum*.[63]

By the twelfth century in Germany, additional dialogue was added so that the hymn incorporated vernacular stanzas. The result was eventually the pre-Reformation chorale *Christ ist erstanden*. Martin Luther's *Christ lag in Todesbanden* is also based on this sequence.

The dozens of imitations that appeared as late as the sixteenth century are evidence of the popularity of *Victimae Paschali laudes*. These include parodies of Martin Luther, one of them an invective from the Roman Catholic perspective, *Pessimas Lutheri fraudes fugiant Christiani* ("Christians are fleeing the most wicked deceptions of Luther"), and one from the Lutheran point of view, *Invictas Martini laudes intonent Christiani* ("Christians are thundering forth the invincible renown of Martin").

The plainsong melody has been associated with this text from the beginning.

☙

The development of religious drama from this sequence is yet another demonstration of the power of incarnation, with a small "I." We human beings experience life not only through those unseen parts of us called "intellect" or "spirit." We see, hear, touch, taste, and move through life. These amazing bodies of ours are given us by God. They are not only temples of God's spirit within us, but are "antennae" which help us to relate to the world around us and to grow in the knowledge and love of God.

The Incarnation, with a capital "I," demonstrated our Creator's intimate understanding of our dependence on our senses for information. The first-century disciples experienced the reality of God when they walked beside Jesus on the dusty roads of Palestine, when they heard his voice, when they saw him on the Mount of Transfiguration or in the Garden of Gethsemane, when they ate with him at the Last Supper, when they carried his corpse from the cross to the garden sepulcher. The untouchable leper, Simon Peter's mother-in-law, and the man born blind, all felt his healing touch.

The power of drama is that we can experience a little of their experience when we watch these sacred stories of the Christian tradition enacted by other human beings. Among my own list of "favorite things" are mystery plays, the medieval dramas enacted on the streets of ancient cities by townspeople and members of the various craftsmen's guilds. In the Easter segment of these plays, still presented from time to time in such venues as the streets of York or the interior of Canterbury Cathedral, ordinary human beings take the roles of the women, the angel, and Jesus. One cannot watch without a physical response: a catch in the throat, a shiver down the spine, a rush of adrenalin.

Drama helps us connect viscerally to the story of the Resurrection. But we need not rely on staged drama to make this connection. The Resurrection is enacted over and over again around us, if we but notice it. We can witness the miracle of people coming to life again after disaster, loss, or illness, or observe the courage of concerned citizens who work to give life back to wetlands or forests or neighborhoods. We ourselves can find new life by contributing our own physical and intellectual gifts—"our souls and bodies"—to this work of resurrection.

When we engage in this work, it may often feel like a battle: against depression, grief, ignorance, and fear. Death and life continue to contend in a stupendous combat. But we are not alone in our endeavor. "Christ indeed from death is risen, / our new life obtaining." Christ has gone before us, and his new life is given to us, so that we ourselves can contribute to the ongoing drama of the Resurrection.

Second Sunday of Easter

Hymn 208   The strife is o'er
Latin, 1695; tr. *Francis Pott (1832–1909)*

This Latin hymn, *Finita iam sunt praelia*, was first printed in Cologne in 1695, but some sources suggest a date as early as the twelfth century.

In 1861, Francis Pott translated the text from the Cologne source for his *Hymns Fitted to the Order of Common Prayer*. A priest born in Southwark and educated at Brasenose College, Oxford, Pott served for many years as rector of a parish in Northill, Bedfordshire, before retiring because of increasing deafness. He devoted the last eighteen years of his life to the improvement of hymnody and worship in the Church of England, and was a charter member of the committee that produced *Hymns Ancient and Modern* in 1861. His *Free Rhythm Psalter*, published in 1898, reflected his special interest in chanting and liturgy.

The tune, "Victory," which is taken from the *Gloria Patri* of Palestrina's *Magnificat Tertii Toni*, has been associated with the text from the beginning.

❧

One of my seminary professors was fond of telling the following story, which he suggested (improbably) was an old "Hasidic tale":

> Judas Iscariot was at the deepest point in hell and saw a small point of light high above him. He started to crawl upward towards the light. The journey was painful and difficult. After a half-million years had passed, he was only a quarter of the way there, but he persisted, crawling always upward towards the light. Another half-million years passed, and the light seemed still to be only a speck in the distance. However, with all his strength, he continued pulling himself towards the light. Another half-million years passed. Now the light seemed infinitesimally closer. Almost exhausted, Judas continued his journey. Finally, after two million years, with almost no strength left, he reached the light and emerged into a room.
>
> In the room was a long table, around which a man dressed in the white garments of the first century was sitting with eleven others. On the table was bread and wine—a meal. The man looked at Judas. "You're finally here! Now we can begin."

I like to think of "The strife is o'er" in terms of this inventive story about God's desire for all humanity to gather at the heavenly banquet table, rather than to remain in the darkness of separation from God.

When we sing "He closed the yawning gates of hell, / the bars from heaven's high portals fell," we can understand this as the literal outcome of the great battle on Golgotha between God and the powers of evil. Some prefer, however, thinking of these phrases in terms of the "yawning gates of hell" that block our minds when we are unable to conceive of God's love and presence. When we come face to face with Love incarnate, as Judas did in my professor's apocryphal story, heaven's high portals, erected by our own ignorance, do indeed fall.

It is from that ignorance and darkness that Christ frees us, demonstrating through the victory of his life God's abundant hospitality and love.

Third Sunday of Easter

Hymn 204   Now the green blade riseth from the buried grain
John Macleod Campbell Crum (1872–1958)

Born in Knutsford, England, Crum was educated at Eton and New College, Oxford. He was ordained a deacon in 1897 and priest in 1900. After a curacy in Darlington, he served for four years as domestic chaplain to the bishop of Oxford, but then returned to the parochial ministry. In 1928, he became a canon of Canterbury Cathedral, where he remained until he retired in 1943. He was especially skilled at writing children's hymns or hymns for special occasions for the parishes he served.

The words of this hymn were written by Crum for the French melody *Noël Nouvelet* for publication in *The Oxford Book of Carols*, published in London in 1928. Crum transformed this old Christmas carol or *noël* into an Easter carol, taking his imagery from John 12:24 ("Very truly, I tell you, unless a grain of wheat falls into the earth and dies, it remains just a single grain; but if it dies, it bears much fruit") and 1 Corinthians 15:37 ("And as for what you sow, you do not sow the body that is to be, but a bare seed, perhaps of wheat or of some other grain").

☙

Ever since I was a small child and learned "The little flowers came through the ground at Eastertime, at Eastertime," the coming to life of nature in the spring has been for me a symbol of the rising of Jesus. This past Easter I decided to explore that metaphor in a new way. When the liturgical procession emerged from the dark church into dazzling sunshine—the first we had seen in over a week—I knew immediately the way I would spend the rest of the day. I celebrated Easter afternoon on my knees in my garden.

I marveled at the transformation beneath me. The daffodils had almost come to the end of their springtime display, but the tulips, which also had been buried unseen all winter, were beginning to open. Forget-me-nots, which had been given me by a now departed friend, had multiplied so that they softened the garden's outlines with a blue nimbus. Lupine seedlings, given to me at another friend's funeral, were pushing through the ground. The Jack-in-the-Pulpits were pushing bravely up through the woodruff, right next to the trillium. The roses were putting forth green shoots on what had looked like dead wood only a few weeks ago. Small shoots of monarda and phlox were poking through the earth. The clematis was winding its vigorous way up the trellis, and, for better or worse, the golden dandelions in the lawn were especially luxuriant. Best of all, I found the vegetable course of our Easter dinner growing in our asparagus bed.

As I mused and weeded, I kept hearing this hymn. I am glad that there is an adult hymn to take the place held by my favorite childhood Easter hymn. The notion that the earth itself celebrates Jesus' resurrection—at least in the Northern hemisphere—helps us recognize the sacramental nature of all things. Springtime beauty is an outward and visible sign of an inward and spiritual grace. It is the Creator's work of art; and it draws us towards the realization that nature itself has integrity, far beyond its usefulness to human beings, and that through its patterns we can learn eternal truths.

At Easter, nature reminds us that the wintry griefs of a human life will finally be melted in the springtime sun, and that death is only a passage to new life. For resurrection is part of nature's design: life always comes again, "like wheat that springeth green."

Fourth Sunday of Easter

Hymn 645, 646   The King of love my shepherd is
Henry Williams Baker (1821–1877)

Born at Belmont House in Vauxhall, London, Baker was the eldest son of Admiral Henry Loraine Baker, a baronet. He was educated at Trinity College, Cambridge, and named vicar of Monkland, near Leominster, in 1844. He succeeded to the baronetcy in 1859, but remained at Monkland until his death.

Baker was a high churchman, who advocated the celibacy of the clergy and produced two devotional books for his parish: *Family Prayers for the Use of those who have to work hard* and a *Daily Text Book*. Baker made a large contribution to the important hymn collection *Hymns Ancient and Modern*, published in London in 1861. As editor, he was prone to making changes in the submitted texts, which led one contributor to quip that *HA&M* should stand for "Hymns Asked for and Mutilated."[64] He also translated Latin hymns, wrote original texts, composed tunes, and engaged the services of other fine hymnwriters, including Monk, Dykes, Elvey, Stainer, and Barnby.

"The King of love my shepherd is," one of the most beloved of hymns, is, like many of the hymns of Luther and Watts, a "Christianized" psalm. The "cup" of Psalm 23 becomes a eucharistic chalice and the cross takes its place with the rod and the staff. The shepherd of the psalm becomes the Good Shepherd of John's gospel (Jn.10:11–18).

John Ellerton wrote in *Church Hymns*, published in London in 1874:

It may interest many to know that the third verse ["Perverse and foolish oft I strayed"] of this lovely hymn, perhaps the most beautiful of all the countless version of Psalm xxiii, was the last audible sentence upon the dying lips of the lamented author. February 12, 1877.[65]

The text is matched to two equally loved tunes, an Irish melody and the tune composed at Baker's request for the appendix of *Hymns Ancient and Modern*.

ᑯ

When I lead workshops in movement as prayer, I almost always use Psalm 23 as a text for interpretation. I usually divide the group into small sub-groups, giving each either a verse of the psalm or a stanza of this hymn. The group's task is to meditate upon the text and then to decide how they will express the words without speaking—in "body language."

This may seem like a game of pious charades, but it is far from that: it is prayer. All language has its origin in a non-verbal part of our brain, what scientists call the "right hemisphere." Religious language, in particular, has its origins in that part of our brain where we "know" but cannot yet express what we know through language, a function of the left hemisphere.

Therefore, expressing Psalm 23 without our usual dependence upon speech can take us into the very origin of thought. This psalm, probably first sung by a king who knew well what it was to be the guardian of a flock of sheep, is based on the experience of God as a shepherd. His experience gave rise to a theological intuition which finally became poetry.

Now that David's poem is the most popular psalm in the

Hebrew Scriptures, how can we recapture this text's experiential quality, its freshness and depth?

In my workshops, the groups gather after a period of time to "pray" their portion of the psalm in the presence of one another. Each time this happens, no matter what the setting or group, Psalm 23 comes alive in a different way.

I once introduced this exercise to a monastic community which included a quite elderly monk who depended on a cane for walking. He immediately rallied his younger brethren, got them down on all fours, and prodded them with his cane, as he nudged them towards "green pastures." That image of the wise yet persistent guidance of an elder remains with me, as a picture of one of the ways we learn to serve God through the length of our days.

I have memories of two women "spreading a table" with careful and attentive hospitality, of two members of a group tenderly anointing one another's foreheads in a healing gesture, and of two men cowering in fear as they traverse "death's dark vale" until a third lays a hand on their shoulders. I no longer just hear this psalm: I see it.

In these workshops, all of us in attendance, whether participants or observers, make a dual journey. One of them is a journey back in time to the origins of the theology ultimately expressed in the poetry. The second is a journey inward, to the hidden place where we ourselves discover anew—and experience with mind, heart, and body—that the Lord God of the psalmist David is our king of love as well.

Fifth Sunday of Easter

Hymn 202   The Lamb's high banquet called to share
Latin, 7th–8th cent.; tr. John Mason Neale (1818–1866)* and
    others

The text *Ad cenam Agni providi* is of unknown origin but was
widely used in both Latin hymn cycles and in the Mozarabic
rite (the name given to the liturgical forms which were in use
in the Iberian Peninsula until the eleventh century.)

The translator, John Mason Neale, comments on the
hymn:

> In order to understand this hymn, we must know
> for whom it was written. It was the custom of the early
> church that baptism should be solemnly administered
> to many *catechumens*, that is, persons who had been
> under instruction and preparation for it, on Easter
> Eve. This hymn then refers in the first place to them
> . . . *The Lamb's high banquet we await*. These newly
> baptized persons were now for the first time about to
> receive the Holy Communion, and therefore truly
> *waiting* for that *high banquet*, "*In snow-white robes*"
> [the *Et stolis albis candidi* of the original], because, at
> baptism, a white garment was given to the persons
> baptized, with words like these: "Take this white ves-
> ture for a token of the innocence which, by God's
> grace, in this holy Sacrament of Baptism, is given unto

---

*For additional biographical information, see *A Closer Walk*, 65–67.

thee and for a sign whereby thou art admonished, so long as thou livest, to give thyself to innocency of living, that after this transitory life thou mayest be partaker of life everlasting."[66]

The text is set to the rhythmic version of its proper chant tune.

℘

I was impressed when I learned in seminary about the baptismal rites of the early church; I could not help but compare the spirit behind them with the comfortable way in which most people today approach baptism, despite efforts to restore the importance of the catechumenate process.

In the beginning, baptism was considered a life-changing threshold. To become a Christian during the time of the persecutions was putting oneself at great risk, and the process of initiation was a serious thing. The rite was not merely a matter of gathering family and godparents around the font and sprinkling water over an infant's head. It required an extensive period of preparation and teaching.

Those who were admitted to training and instruction preparatory to baptism, which always happened at the Paschal Mass, were called *catechumens*. During the time that preceded their baptism, they were allowed to sit in an assigned place in the church, but were solemnly dismissed before the Eucharist proper began. "Let the catechumens depart. Let no catechumens remain!"

It was only when they were baptized that the new Christians heard, for the first time, the *Sursum Corda* ("Lift up your hearts") which precedes the *Sanctus*, or the words of consecration we know so well, "This is my body; this is my blood." Arrayed "in garments white and fair," they were finally full members of the Christian community.

It was a personal passage like the historic passage of the Israelites through the Red Sea, from captivity to freedom. Like the Israelites, they were free to make that passage because of a death.

> Then Moses called all the elders of Israel and said to them, "Go, select lambs for your families and slaughter the passover lamb. Take a bunch of hyssop, dip it in the blood that is in the basin, and touch the lintel and the two doorposts with the blood in the basin. . . . The Lord will pass through to strike down the Egyptians; when he sees the blood on the lintel and on the two doorposts, the Lord will pass over that door and will not allow the destroyer to enter your houses to strike you down." (Ex.12:21–23)

For early Christians, baptism had the same element of urgency. Like the Israelites following Moses from the security of known slavery into the unknown territory that lay beyond the Red Sea, they left comfort behind and courageously faced an unknown future.

Ad cenam Agni providi reminds us that the death of Jesus was a passport to freedom, and that the heavenly food of the Eucharist, like the unleavened bread the Israelites took with them on their flight, is our perpetual nourishment, giving us courage for what lies ahead of us. We celebrate this every Sunday, as we remember the Paschal mystery: the passage through death, from bondage to freedom.

Sixth Sunday of Easter

Hymn 513   **Like the murmur of the dove's song**
Carl P. Daw, Jr. (b. 1944) *

During the preparation of *The Hymnal 1982*, the Text Committee received many hymn requests based primarily on attraction to a very fine tune rather than to the words associated with it. This was the case with the tune "Bridegroom" by Peter Cutts, which had been written for a text full of images of monarchy which the committee considered inappropriate for modern American congregations. They therefore asked Carl P. Daw, Jr., then a student at the School of Theology, The University of the South, in Sewanee, Tennessee, to write a text to fit the tune.

Daw played over the tune repeatedly and became convinced that the final phrase of the music expressed a prayer for the coming of the Holy Spirit. With the concluding refrain, "Come, Holy Spirit, come," in mind, he then used each stanza to consider different aspects of this petition.

He writes:

> The opening phrase is derived from my recollection of the following passage concerning the Holy Spirit in Louis Evely's book, *A Religion for Our Time*: I have learned that the image of a dove was chosen not because of the shape of the bird, but because of the moan. The dove murmurs all the time. It is because the Holy Spirit

---

*For additional biographical information, see 66.

moans all the time that he is represented under the form of a dove; it is a verbal and not a plastic image. The Spirit helps us in our weakness, for we do not know how to pray as we ought, but the Spirit himself intercedes for us "with sighs too deep for words." (Rom. 8:26)

The first stanza presents both the aural and the visual aspects of the dove as a symbol of the Holy Spirit, as well as the other two traditional images of wind and fire, thereby portraying the "how" of the Spirit's coming. The second stanza turns to the "where" aspect, and affirms that the Spirit is a corporate gift to the whole church. The third stanza concerns itself with the purpose for which the Spirit is given (the "why"): for reconciliation, prayer, divine power, and quiet confidence. Like the ancient hymn "Veni Sancte Spiritus," this new text pulls together diverse images of both the Holy Spirit and the People of God in an attempt to suggest the scope of divine power and the depth of human need.[67]

❧

I am familiar with the murmur of the dove's song. Two mourning doves are regular visitors to the ground underneath our birdfeeder, where they enjoy the seed spilled by smaller birds. I always know when they are in the vicinity, because of their haunting song. I know when they are heading for our feeder because of the unique whirring sound of their flight, like the vibration of a plucked viola string. They are beautiful birds, their curvaceous bodies covered in feathers of subtle beiges and greys. They are also peaceful birds. They do not squabble like the blue jays or sparrows, but seem to take pleasure in just sitting in the crabapple tree near the feeder, surveying the activity below.

I have also had experience with the wind's rush. I remember standing on the shore of the English Channel during a violent storm when our youngest child was nine. Fortunately, his hand was in mine when a blast of wind swept from the sea with such force that he would have been pulled out of my grasp if I had not been holding on tightly.

When we enjoy a wood fire on a cold evening, I like to watch the initial small flame ignite the logs, until there is a blaze of warmth. I remember sitting in front of the fireplace in my childhood home, watching it as children today watch television. When we try to describe the Holy Spirit, the dove, the wind, and the flame make up the trinity of ways we experience its presence and power.

Often it is like those faithful doves in my back yard, brooding over the activity here on earth and constantly murmuring prayerful reassurances to our timid souls. The Spirit is there even when I have forgotten God, just as the mourning doves are present in our neighborhood whether I see them or not.

But sometimes it is more insistent, like a sudden strong wind. There are times when the Spirit literally sweeps us off our feet, in order to deposit us elsewhere. At these times, the Spirit seems to bring, not peace, but chaos. But it is a chaos out of which something new is born.

Or the Holy Spirit may be like fire, its warmth fanning the small flame of a thought until it becomes a conflagration in the form of something we feel impelled and inspired to do.

We cannot predict which symbol will best describe the Holy Spirit's next visitation to us: the dove, the wind, or the flame. We do not know whether its gift will be healing and peace, or an initiative for a difficult new ministry. But as individuals, and as members of Christ's Body the church, we dare to desire its coming into our midst. Come, Holy Spirit, come.

Ascension Day

Hymn 220, 221   O Lord Most High, eternal King
Medieval Latin; sts. 1–3, tr. *John Mason Neale (1818–1866)*;
st. 4, tr. *Laurence Housman (1865–1959)*

Both the date and the authorship of this Latin hymn, *Aeterne rex altissime, Redemptor*, are unknown, although it is first found in manuscripts of the tenth century. The final stanza is a doxology associated with several medieval Ascension hymns. In Roman use, the hymn is assigned to the Office of Reading for the Ascension.

The attribution of the translation to F. Bland Tucker and Benjamin Webb in *The Hymnal 1982* is erroneous; rather, Tucker reworked the translations by John Mason Neale and Laurence Housman, the English poet, playwright, and author.

Two musical settings are provided: a medieval plainsong associated with the text from the beginning, and a soaring early-twentieth-century English tune.

൚

"And angels wonder when they see / how changed is our humanity." The picture this text brings to my mind is quite different from most of the depictions of the Ascension. It is the view above the scene: the sight of the angel faces alight with their joy and surprise that there seems to be hope for the human race, after all.

For it is not just Jesus who was changed at the Ascension. It was the idea of our capacity for goodness. Jesus, the man who most perfectly represented what it means to be a human "made in God's image," holds before us the possibility of holiness.

That seems like a tall order for us. Some years ago, I bought a book on the subject just because the title seemed so improbable. In that book, *Holiness*, the author Donald Nicholl holds before us this surprising ideal as a life's work:

> The most difficult task is to begin. We are all aware of this, whether the task is getting out of bed in the morning or writing a long-overdue letter. But since this matter of holiness is essentially paradoxical it is true that beginning in holiness is also quite simple because we can begin at any time and at any place.[68]

We begin where we are. It is as simple as that. Gandhi said, "If you don't find God in the very next person you meet it is a waste of time looking for him further."[69] As Nicholl points out, Gandhi had the ability to shake people into beginning their spiritual work through the means of short and unforgettable sayings. He was like Rabi'a, a Muslim mystic who lived in Baghdad a thousand years ago, who replied to a disciple who asked her the first step she should take in order to achieve the virtue of patience: "Stop complaining."[70]

There is an Indian saying that "If you take one step towards God then God will take ten steps towards you."[71] It is another way of saying that holiness is not something that humans can achieve through their own efforts, but only through the grace of God. But it doesn't happen unless we try. And we need first to discover that the risen and ascended Christ is indeed our joy, and that the ideal of a holy life he has shown to us can be our choice as well. Only one thing is necessary: to begin.

Seventh Sunday of Easter

Hymn 315   Thou, who at thy first Eucharist didst pray
William Harry Turton (1856–1938)

William Henry Turton was born in Peshawur, India. He was educated at Clifton College, Bristol, where he received the Royal Geographical Society's gold medal, and at the Royal Military Academy, Woolwich, where he received the Pollock medal. At the age of twenty, he was commissioned in the Royal Engineers, and attained the rank of lieutenant colonel in 1902. He participated in the South African War from 1900 to 1902, and was named a Companion of the Distinguished Service Order. In 1905, he retired to live in Bristol.

His various publications include three series of twelve hymns, published between 1880 and 1883, each under the title *A Few Hymns written by a Layman*. Evidence of the diversity of its interests are his other publications: *The Truth of Christianity*; *The Plantagenet Ancestry*; and *The Marine Shells of Port Alfred*.

The text "Thou, who at thy first Eucharist didst pray" was included in the first set of *A Few Hymns written by a Layman*. It was sung for the first time at the anniversary service of the English Church Union held at St. Mary Magdalene Church, Munster Square, in June of 1881.

The text is matched with a meditative tune by Orlando Gibbons.

℘

What would it mean for all God's church to "be for ever one?" Would it mean that the differences that distinguish Roman

Catholics from Lutherans, Eastern Orthodox from Presbyterians, and Episcopalians from Baptists would be obliterated?

This seems not only an unattainable goal, but an undesirable one. The religious diversity that enriches Christianity can be compared to the cultural variety that enriches life in the United States. Sociologists point out that the "melting pot" is neither an accurate image for the diversity of United States citizens, nor a healthy goal for the nation's future.

Alternative images have been offered. One is a "stew," in which each ingredient can be identified—chunks of meat, potatoes, carrots, onions, even the odd bayleaf—unlike my recipe for split pea soup, which instructs me to put the cooked ingredients into the blender for the finishing touches.

Or, perhaps, should we continue to look in our kitchen for metaphors, we should consider a salad. In one large wooden bowl, I like to toss together various kinds of greens, and other vegetables such as tomatoes, cucumbers, and onions, into a flavorful whole.

I think of yet another image which has remained with me ever since I saw Stephen Sondheim's imaginative musical *Sunday in the Park with George* on Broadway. The story is based on the French painter Georges Seurat, who created wonderful paintings by dabbing small dots of various colors on the canvas. His theory, called "pointillism," is based on what happens to the human eye when it sees different colors placed next to one another: the many dots become one color, which glows in a way that a flat expanse of one shade of paint could never do.

When the curtain opens, the audience sees before them a scrim on which is depicted one of Seurat's best known paintings, *A Sunday on the Grand Jatte*, depicting a park on the banks of the Seine on a sunny Sunday afternoon, where

Parisians stroll, relax, and daydream. If you look closely—or go to visit the painting itself at the Art Institute of Chicago—you see that no figure is outlined: the entire painting is like a mosaic of dots of different colors. The river is "blue purple yellow red water" and under the feet of the strollers in the park is "green purple yellow red grass."[72]

Later in the play, Georges is painting in his studio and sings a song, "Color and Light," which describes his quest to apply specks of unmixed pigments to the canvas so that they can combine optically in the viewer's eye, creating a light-filled vision.

"Color and light" might be a good motto for the ecumenical movement, as well as for the differences within a denomination or parish. Our differences can be either divisive or they can be exciting—like the color and light of Seurat's paintings. To make it possible for the latter to happen, we need not give up our cherished beliefs or even say that they do not matter. Instead, we need only to let go of our desire to force our beliefs on others. There are serious issues which threaten to divide us. But when we refuse to become enemies, when we dare to talk with one another, we are like the dots of bright orange or pink or red that Seurat carefully placed on his canvases, living side by side.

It is, I think, the only way that Christians today can truly be "forever one." Each dot retains its integrity; but together, they are a new creation, and a beautiful one: color and light.

The Day of Pentecost

Hymn 229   Spirit of mercy, truth, and love
Anon., *Psalms, Hymns, and Anthems,* 1774

This anonymous eighteenth-century English text is an example of hymnody that came from an unlikely source: the charity houses of the mid-eighteenth century. These institutions, which ministered to the sick, the poor, and the orphaned, had been created in response to the rising social concerns that had found expression in the ministry of John and Charles Wesley.

The text made its first appearance in 1774 at the Foundling Hospital in London. This orphanage, founded by Thomas Coram in 1738, developed a distinctive reputation for music that played a role in the rehabilitation of the children. In addition, the Hospital held special benefit concerts for the financing of its work. There are many descriptions, in writings of that period, of the effect produced by the massed children's voices.

The chapel was noted not only for its musical services but also for performances of sacred oratorios. This was due in part to the influence of the composer George Frideric Handel, who had a long association with the Foundling Hospital. In 1749, he arranged a benefit to raise money for the new chapel building, for which he composed an anthem, "Blessed are they that consider the poor." He donated an organ to the completed chapel and gave the inaugural organ recital in April 1750, which had to be repeated because of the number of people who had to be turned away. Later Handel was to conduct annual performances of his *Messiah* in the chapel, and he made the institution a major beneficiary in his will.

A collection of sixteen hymns for use in the chapel was published in 1774, entitled *Psalms, Hymns and Anthems used in the Chapel of the Hospital for the Maintenance of Exposed and Deserted Young Children*. Among them was "Spirit of mercy, truth, and love." The hymn soon entered into many different hymn collections.

The text is paired with a new tune by a contemporary American composer.

ᘓᗏ

In proper trinitarian style, the anonymous author of this hymn understands the Spirit's influence to be threefold: mercy, truth, and love. At Pentecost, we celebrate these gifts of the Spirit, given to the gathered church. They are a sign that not only do we know God as a bearer of mercy, truth, and love, but we ourselves are to become people distinguished by these three qualities.

If members of the Christian family, like medieval royalty and aristocracy, were to adopt a coat of arms emblazoned with words and symbols, we might do well to inscribe these three: mercy, truth, and love.

We would hope that anyone observing these qualities would be able to identify us as belonging to Christ, just as people were able to identify a knight's family by the coat of arms that decorated his armor. These symbols also provided important information in an age when few people were literate, because they were used to prove the authenticity of various important documents.

However, we do not actually need to wear our coat of arms to prove our identification as Christians. Rather, it is emblazoned on our hearts and in every decision we make.

When these words become part of our interior heraldry, they help to identify us. Mercy, truth, and love are revealed in our capacity for compassion, integrity, and desire for the well-being of other people.

In this era, the many different mottos emblazoned on people's hearts are revealed through their actions. It is a revelatory exercise to read the newspapers or look at television with the goal of identifying the probable "coats of arms" of the people in the news. Even a week's attention could provide a whole book of modern heraldry.

In this age of self-indulgence, some of the mottos may be depressing. "The problems of other people are not my business." "A little lie or two won't hurt." "My own well-being comes first."

But we may find ourselves encouraged, as well. It is likely that the woman who gave a kidney to save a stranger has "love" emblazoned on her coat of arms, and that the politician who had the courage to admit wrongdoing has "truth" written there. We, who aspire to the same mottos, would hope that we will be similarly recognized by others, as being bearers of the Spirit's gifts, given at Pentecost, and throughout our lives.

Trinity Sunday

Hymn 362   Holy, holy, holy!
*Reginald Heber (1783–1826)**

"Holy, holy, holy!", the best known of Reginald Heber's hymns, was first published in his *A Selection of Psalms and Hymns for the Parish Church of Banbury*, in the year of his

---

*For additional biographical information, see *A Closer Walk*, 37–38.

death. A year later, it appeared posthumously in his *Hymns written and adapted to the Weekly Church Service of the Year*.

The hymnologist Percy Dearmer writes that Heber's unusual 11 12.12 10 metre perhaps inaugurated the increasing width of metrical range in later hymnody. He adds:

> It was the more valuable because in the Victorian books there were so few hymns about God; and this, free from all subjectivity, filled a large gap, expressing the pure spirit of worship in stately language. . . .[73]

The hymn's imagery is based on the fourth chapter of the Book of Revelation, in which John describes his vision of the Lamb of God upon a throne before which is "something like a sea of glass, like crystal." (Rev.4:6) In front stand four living creatures, who sing without ceasing, "Holy, holy, holy, the Lord God the Almighty, who was and is and is to come." (Rev.4:8) As the creatures sing, twenty-four elders "worship the one who lives forever and ever; they cast their crowns before the throne." (Rev.4:10)

"Holy, holy, holy" is also the song of the seraphim in Isaiah's vision in Isaiah 6:2–3: "Holy, holy, holy is the Lord of hosts; the whole earth is full of his glory." It is also, of course, the origin of the "Sanctus" in the Eucharist.

Heber's "Holy, holy, holy" was the poet Tennyson's favorite hymn: "Of hymns I like Heber's 'Holy, holy, holy' better than most; and it is in a fine metre too."[74] It was sung at Tennyson's funeral in Westminster Abbey in April 1892.

The music, universally accepted as *the* tune for this text, was written especially for Heber's poem, and is often regarded as the "archetypal Victorian hymn tune."[75]

❧

Erik Routley writes of this hymn:

> In that word "Holy" is epitomized the most august of Old Testament lines of thought and experience. For men of that day, the "holy" was primarily the untouchable.... A holy thing was a thing you might not touch; a holy mountain was a mountain you might not climb; a holy place was a place you might not enter ... [I]n that delicate reticence and courtesy which is part of the texture of the religious life at its most mature, you keep away from something because you love it and feel unworthy to come too near it.[76]

When I was growing up, the only people allowed in the sanctuary of our parish church were the priests, the acolytes, and the members of the altar guild—the only females privileged to go beyond the altar rail, provided they wore blue veils on their heads. This was a place that was so sacred that even kneeling to receive communion sent chills down the spine. When, in my early forties, I became a lay reader and chalice bearer and went beyond the altar rail, it felt at first like breaking a taboo. And yet how I loved doing it!

When I went to seminary, I understood a bit more about what I had experienced, when a professor, in speaking about God, used the phrase, *Mysterium Tremendum et Fascinans*, which is translated, "Mystery both terrifying and fascinating." I, of course, was far from the first to experience both the fear and the attraction of holiness. Even in the Hebrew Scriptures, the holiness of God was a paradox. God was experienced as both awesome and mighty and also as familiar and near. God was too transcendent to be represented in drawing or sculpture, but was personal enough to be represented through stories and word-pictures.

The paradox of God's holiness was made more complex by Jesus, born of a human mother in Bethlehem, and by the event of Pentecost, when it became clear that God was working in the world. In an attempt to describe their experience to the world in a way that others could understand intellectually, the early church struggled with these expressions of the divine holiness and forged the doctrine of the Trinity.

And yet this doctrine remains a challenge. It makes us stretch our intellects to the utmost limit, and conclude that we can never understand the doctrine with our finite minds.

That is why "Holy, holy, holy," does us such a service. As Routley says, it lays ". . . all the emphasis on the wonder and majesty of [the Trinity] and none whatever on the intellectual athleticism of it. . . . The very shakiness and disjointedness in the hymn are a kind of humility." The text, "so magnificently incoherent, so ejaculatory in its diction . . ." clothed in the "mysterious shot-silk colours of the book of *Revelation*,"[77] accentuates our awe at the holy. We do not need to figure out the doctrine of the Trinity; we need only to sing.

Proper 1: The Sunday closest to May 11

Same as on the Sixth Sunday after Epiphany
(see page 60)

Proper 2: The Sunday closest to May 18

Same as on the Seventh Sunday after Epiphany
(see page 63)

Proper 3: The Sunday closest to May 25

Same as on the Eighth Sunday after Epiphany
(see page 66)

Proper 4: The Sunday closest to June 1

Hymn 626   Lord, be thy word my rule
Christopher Wordsworth (1807–1885)*

In 1862, Christopher Wordsworth published *The Holy Year*, a collection of hymns based on the liturgical year. The volume has been an ongoing source of texts for hymnals ever since.

"Lord, be thy word my rule" appeared in the sixth edition of *The Holy Year*, with the title "at Confirmation." It is based on King Charles I's prayer "O Lord, make thy way plain before me. Let thy glory be my end, thy word my rule; and then, thy will be done."[78] Erik Routley calls Wordsworth's hymn "one of the shortest hymns in common use, and one of the most perfect."[79]

The text is set to an uncomplicated nineteenth-century tune.

∽

Several times I have visited Little Gidding in Cambridgeshire, the site of the seventeenth-century community founded by Nicholas Ferrar. On my first visit, I remember standing with a

---

*For additional biographical information, see *A Closer Walk*, 134–136 and *New Every Morning*, 40–41.

resident looking out at the peaceful farmland that surrounded us on every side. She pointed out over the rolling fields: "That is the way the king came."

In my mind's eye, I saw Charles I, a fugitive from the Parliamentary forces, riding over those hills in the dead of night on March 2, 1646 to seek sanctuary with his friends. Her comment transformed my picture of this ill-fated King of England from a cardboard figure in my history books into a living, breathing human being.

Imagining the figure fleeing for his life across the Cambridgeshire countryside made me want to learn more about the about the shy and reserved boy who was to inherit the crown in 1625. Although Charles had been tutored by a Scottish Calvinist as a boy, as king he was a high churchman who believed in free will rather than predestination. He appointed clergy who preferred ritual and prayers from the prayer book to long sermons and extemporaneous prayer—a taste shared by most of today's Episcopalians. Unfortunately, not everyone shared his opinions or his policies. He fell into the hands of the Roundhead army in 1647, and in 1649 was publicly executed by Cromwell's supporters outside Whitehall Palace in London.

His prayer, "O Lord, make thy way plain before me. Let thy glory be my end, thy word my rule; and then, thy will be done," must have been often on his lips. How difficult it must be to juggle the desire to follow God's rule with the exigencies of oneself being the ruler!

When I was little, I was very confused about what a "ruler" was. When I heard the story of Joseph in Egypt and learned that the boy sold by his jealous brothers had eventually become a "ruler," all I could picture was that strip of wood marked off in inches that nestled in my pencil box.

My childish image may not be too far from the truth. People in responsibility help their communities to "measure" themselves against standards that contribute to the well-being of those communities. We do this as parents, teachers, executives, religious leaders, and—each one of us—as engaged citizens. Charles I, in his prayer, reminds us of where we can find the best standard against which to measure our common life: "Lord, be thy word my rule; / in it may I rejoice; / thy glory be my aim, / thy holy will my choice."

Proper 5: *The Sunday closest to June 8*

Hymn 255   We sing the glorious conquest
John Ellerton (1826–1893)

John Ellerton was born in London and educated at King William's College, the Isle of Man, and Trinity College, Cambridge. After his ordination, he was appointed curate at St. Nicholas', Brighton, where he began his career as an author by writing hymns for the children of the parish. While he was vicar of Crewe Green, he compiled *Hymns for Schools and Bible Classes* (1859). He was one of the editors and writers for *Church Hymns* (1874), for which Arthur Sullivan was music editor.

Later, while he was rector of Hinstock, he wrote the article on "Hymns" for the *Dictionary of Christian Antiquities* and co-edited *Children's Hymns and School Prayers*. He eventually became the SPCK Tract Committee's authority on matters of poetry and music, wrote historical notes on hymnological matters for many publications, and continued to write and revise his own texts. Ellerton was greatly influenced by the radical theologian J. Frederick Denison Maurice, who was actively interested in the application of Christian principles to social reform.

The original version of this hymn was written to provide a text for the celebration of the Conversion of St. Paul in *Church Hymns*. It is based on the story of Paul's conversion in Acts 9:1–22, 22:4–16, and 26:9–18, as well as Paul's own account in Galations 1:13–17.

The text is matched with a well-known German tune.

⌘

Most of the stained glass windows in our local Episcopal church were created by an artist I knew when I was in college. Margaret was an art history student who undertook as her master's project to demonstrate the craft of medieval stained glass windows, using the church's unadorned windows as her palette. She thought not only artistically but theologically. At the rear of the church she placed six windows portraying prophets, each of whom she studied in depth before trying to translate their voices into stained glass. At each side of the nave, windows depict aspects of the faith, among them Creation and Fall, Redemption, Sanctification, and Judgment.

When Margaret came to the window on the left side of the church closest to the altar, she chose the story of Paul, beginning when the man Saul, not yet re-named, "persecuted the church of God violently and tried to destroy it." The images of the stoning of Stephen under Saul's supervision prompted a former organist, who also bore the martyr's name, to point out that the persecution of his namesake, directly across the chancel from the organ console, was a compelling object of meditation during sermons.

The figures in Saul's story interweave, but the eye inevitably focuses just above the center of the window where Margaret has depicted his vision on the Damascus road:

> Meanwhile Saul, still breathing threats and murder against the disciples of the Lord, went to the high priest and asked him for letters to the synagogues at Damascus, so that if he found any who belonged to the Way, men or women, he might bring them bound to Jerusalem. Now as he was going along and approaching Damascus, suddenly a light from heaven flashed around him. He fell to the ground and heard a voice saying to him, "Saul, Saul, why do you persecute me?" He asked, "Who are you, Lord?" The reply came, "I am Jesus, whom you are persecuting. But get up and enter the city, and you will be told what you are to do." The men who were traveling with him stood speechless because they heard the voice but saw no one. Saul got up from the ground, and though his eyes were open, he could see nothing; so they led him by the hand and brought him into Damascus. (Acts 9:1–8)

The figure of Jesus in Margaret's window is not, as one would expect, a human figure surrounded by light. Instead, Margaret surprises the viewer by representing the one whom Saul is persecuting by a large oblong of opaque black glass surrounded by a yellow aura. Saul, she suggests, is not able to make out the source of the voice that speaks within him, for it is a source so dazzling that it blinds him.

Theologians use the word "apophatic" to describe our perceptions of God that are beyond images and description. Margaret, an astute lay theologian, might well have described this visual representation of Paul's interlocutor as "apophatic art."

Her representation reminds me of how often we are blind to the presence of Christ in the world around us. In our ignorance, we may, in fact, be persecuting him: through unjust political stances that harm our needy brothers and sisters, in our destruction of wild habitat through greed, and in a myriad of other ways in which we hurl the stones of indifference and narrow-mindedness.

We, like Saul, do this because we just have not gotten the picture yet. May we, like him, be blessed with a vision that helps us realize that we need to recognize God in unexpected places, and become apostles of hope to all the known world.

Proper 6: The Sunday closest to June 15

Hymn 691   My faith looks up to thee
Ray Palmer (1808–1887)

Ray Palmer was born in Rhode Island, the son of a judge. His early life was spent in Boston, where he was for some time a clerk in a dry goods store. There, he joined the Park Street Congregational Church on what was called "Brimstone Corner," caught its evangelizing fervor, and decided to become a minister. He spent three years at Phillips Andover Academy, then entered Yale College, where he graduated in 1830. To support himself while studying theology, he taught at girls' schools for the following five years, first in New York City, then in New Haven. In 1835, he was ordained and became pastor of Central Congregational Church in Bath, Maine, where he served until appointed to First Congregational Church in Albany in 1850. Towards the end of his career he was corresponding secretary to the American Congregational Union.

Palmer's publications include fifteen original hymns and translations from Latin in the Andover Academy's *Sabbath Hymns Book*, *Sacred Pieces* (1865), *Hymns of My Holy Hours* (1868), and *The Complete Poetical Works* (1876).

"My faith looks up to thee," the first and best-known of his hymns, was written in 1830 when Palmer was only twenty-two years of age. At the time, Palmer was teaching in a "select school for young ladies" in New York the year after his graduation from Yale. The author writes, "I gave form to what I felt, by writing, with little effort, the stanzas. I recollect I wrote them with very tender emotion, and ended the last line with tears."[80]

A year later, he met Lowell Mason on a street in Boston; Mason mentioned that he was publishing a hymnal and invited him to submit some hymns. The two friends stepped into a store and Palmer made a copy of the words of this hymn for Mason. It appeared in *Spiritual Songs for Social Worship*, published in 1831. The hymn has been translated into many languages, including Arabic, Chinese, Tahitian, Tamil, and Marathi.

The text is set to the tune composed for it by Lowell Mason.

ᦗ

"My faith looks up to thee" is the product of an American Congregationalism that was the inheritor of the English evangelical tradition. It is no wonder, then, that there is a deep undercurrent of Calvinism in the text, especially in the final stanza, which has been omitted in *The Hymnal 1982*:

> When ends life's transient dream,
> When death's cold, sullen stream
> Shall o'er me roll;

> Blest Saviour, then in love,
> Fear and distrust remove;
> O bear me safe above,
> A ransomed soul.[81]

The hymn scholar Lioney Adey accuses Palmer of self-indulgence:

> His adjectives here betray desire for a love quite other than the "living fire" of God's love, a return to infantile dependence. As if knowingly indebted, like so many nineteenth-century children, to a mother who had nearly "died for" him at his birth, he longs not to "stray" from the universal parent, but be borne "safe above" from "life's transient dream."[82]

Despite Adey's criticism, the fact remains that the hymn is beloved by many who are neither Congregationalists nor Calvinists, and that it has found a place in our hymnal. I find it very helpful to place it in a developmental context rather than in a theological one, imagining the life of a young man only twenty-two years old.

Because I live in a college community, I know many young men and women who are in their very early twenties. I am struck by the fact that college students live in two worlds simultaneously. Most of them are still dependent on their parents financially, but they also long for independence. When I taught a class in stress reduction in the college a few years ago, I asked the students to list sources of stress in their lives. Not a few of them wrote about the difficulty of moving back and forth between life at college, where they were viewed as adults, and life at home, where they were treated like, and sometimes felt like, children. These students live in an in-between time, wanting to be entirely responsible for their own lives, and yet not quite equipped to do so, either financially or, often, psychologically, because well-meaning adults are often too eager to pick up the pieces.

Parents I know well tell of arriving for their son's graduation, only to discover that he would not be permitted to march in the graduation procession because he had neglected to obtain a necessary professorial signature which would certify he had undertaken a certain winter project. The determined mother called the registrar late in the evening and arranged for an audience first thing on graduation morning, then tracked down the professor for the necessary signature.

It was not many years later that the son lived on his own, in a community far from his parents, and, if such oversights occurred, his parents neither knew or could do anything about them.

I would not be surprised if such tales can be told by many parents and professors; I am sure my parents could have described situations in which I provided them with similar dilemmas.

Ray Palmer, of course, lived in a different era, when independence was forced upon him early. But his blend of what Adey calls his "fluency, egoism, and nostalgia"[83] still lives in young people moving between adolescence and adulthood. In fact, it lives in each of us occasionally, at whatever age. From adolescence to old age, we all experience times when our hearts feel faint, our souls are weighed down with guilt, and our courage challenged by darkness and sorrow. When we come face to face with our dependence, our only solution is to look upwards to our Lord in faith, asking for help.

Proper 7: The Sunday closest to June 22

Hymn 10   New every morning is the love
John Keble (1792–1866)

John Keble was born in Fairford, Gloucestershire, and received his early education in his father's vicarage. At fourteen, he won a scholarship to Corpus Christi College, Oxford. After a brilliant career there, he was elected, at the age of 19, to one of the coveted Fellowships of Oriel. Ordained deacon in 1815 and priest in 1816, he became a tutor at Oriel, but he resigned in 1823 to assist his father in his country parish in the Cotswolds.

There he composed the poems, which, at the insistence of close friends, he published in 1827 as *The Christian Year*. He wrote in the volume about his hope that the reader "will find assistance from it in bringing his own thoughts and feelings into more entire unison with those recommended and exemplified in the Prayer Book."[84] The book is now regarded as a classic collection of religious poetry and considered "an expression of a rare and refined sensibility, imbued with the spirit of both Scripture and the Book of Common Prayer."[85]

In 1831 he was elected professor of poetry at Oxford. With many of his circle of friends, he became increasingly concerned about what he considered to be the dangers threatening the Church of England from the reforming and liberal movements. On July 14, 1833, Keble preached before the university a sermon on "National Apostasy", directed especially against the suppression of ten Irish bishoprics. This "Assizes Sermon" was the spark that ignited the Oxford Movement. His colleagues began to publish a series of *Tracts for the Times*, recalling the church to its ancient sacramental heritage. The movement drew on the skills of several great churchmen: it has been said that "John Henry Newman was the intellectual leader of the Movement, Edward Bouverie Pusey was the prophet of its devotional life, and John Keble was its pastoral inspiration."[86]

In 1836, Keble became the vicar of Hursley, near Winchester, where he remained as a devoted parish priest for the rest of his life. The ecclesiastical historian Frank Leslie Cross writes, "His beauty of character impressed all who came into contact with him, and his advice on spiritual matters, always given with great diffidence, was widely sought after."[87] In 1870, Keble College, Oxford, was founded in his memory.

"New every morning is the love" was part of a poem written on September 20, 1822, headed "Morning," which begins "Hues of the rich unfolding morn," from Keble's *The Christian Year.* The text is inspired by Lamentations 3:22–33:

> The steadfast love of the LORD never ceases,
>   his mercies never come to an end;
> they are new every morning;
>   great is your faithfulness.

The poem is matched with an American folk hymn.

&

Some people waken quickly, ready to spring out of bed. I do not. I "come to" slowly, which gives me the advantage of noticing the sensations of once again being conscious, "restored to life and power and thought."

Sometimes I am aware first of sounds. That is the case, of course, when I set my alarm clock and its insistent jangle forces me to wake. But I prefer gentler sounds: the wind blowing snow against our windows in the winter; the birds' dawn chorus in springtime; the rumble of summer thunder; the regular breathing of my husband, still asleep beside me.

As the sounds pull me from sleep, I become aware of my muscles, inactive too long, and of their need to move. I enjoy the deliciousness of the first long stretch of my legs and arms and torso. I notice my own breathing as my lungs expand.

It is only then that thoughts begin to surface from the dark chaos of sleep. Perhaps I remember a dream, especially when it has been interrupted by the sounds which wake me, or I think of what I need to do that day, or remember someone who has been on my mind.

But, mostly, my first thought is, "Another day of life. Thank you, God."

The familiar saying "This is the first day of the rest of your life" is not a sentimental slogan, but a profound truth. Every morning we have the opportunity to begin anew. Our "up-rising" each morning is a reminder that we can be born again, and again and again, as we emerge from the womb of night.

We do not know what moments lie ahead of us each day; they are the treasure as yet hidden from us. But we do know that, like the precious jewels which rich pilgrims brought to medieval shrines, they are our best offering to God.

The "trivial round" can be our offering: our faithful accomplishment of the most ordinary tasks can be hallowed just by our attitude, if "on our daily course our mind / be set to hallow all we find." Unexpected challenges will give us an arena in which to emulate Christ's self-sacrificing love. If the day brings sadness or conflict, our cares will be softened by the prayer that draws us nearer to our crucified Lord.

I have a friend who tells me he spends part of his morning prayer time with his appointment book in hand, holding each activity of the forthcoming day before God. Keble would have applauded him, for our first thoughts and prayers each day help us, in the hours that follow, to remember God's gracious love, new every morning, again and again.

Proper 8: The Sunday closest to June 29

Hymn 564,565   He who would valiant be
Percy Dearmer (1867–1936)*, after John Bunyan (1628–1688)

John Bunyan was born in Elstow, England, the son of a tinker. He learned reading and writing at the village school, took up his father's trade, and was drafted into the Parliamentary Army. He became an avid student of Scripture and, in 1653, joined a Nonconformist (Baptist) church in Bedford. He was soon inspired with the resolve to become a preacher so that "he might mend the souls of people as well as their pots and pans."[88]

During the Restoration, Bunyan was arrested for preaching in a "conventicle," or illegal meeting. When promised pardon if he would stop preaching, he replied, "If I were out of prison today, I would preach the gospel again tomorrow, by the help of God."[89] He spent most of the next twelve years in Bedford gaol. He wrote nine books during the first half of this period. The principal work was *Grace Abounding to the Chief of Sinners*, which was soon followed by *A Confession of my Faith, and a Reason of my Practice*, a spiritual biography.

---

*For biographical information, see 72–73.

Released by the Declaration of Indulgence of Charles II in 1672, he was called as pastor to the Bedford church, which met in a barn. From there, he preached throughout the shire so effectively that he was dubbed "Bishop Bunyan."

When Parliament revoked the Declaration of Indulgence, Bunyan lost his license to preach, but he persisted and was soon jailed again. The original warrant for his arrest reads:

> yett once John Bunnyon of your said Towne, Tynker, hath divers times within one month last past in contempt of his Majestie's good laws preached or teached at a Conventicle meeteing or assembly under colour or pretense of exercise of Religion in other manner than according to the Liturgie or Practice of the Church of England.[90]

During this period in jail, he is thought to have finished the first part of *The Pilgrim's Progress*, which he had begun during his first imprisonment. The first part of the book was published in 1678, and the completed work was published in 1685.

The Pilgrim's Progress is an allegory which takes the form of a dream by the author: "As I walk'd through the wilderness of this world, I lighted on a certain place where there was a Den, and I laid me down in that place to sleep; and as I slept, I dreamed a Dream."[91] (It is likely that the "Den" refers to the tiny gate-house prison half way across the narrow bridge that spanned the river Ouse in Bedford.)

The book is the story of Christian, who flees from the City of Destruction and travels as a pilgrim through such landscapes as the Slough of Despond, the Valley of Humiliation, the Vanity Fair, Doubting Castle, and the Delectable Mountains, until he finally reaches the Celestial City.

Part II tells the story of Christian's wife, Christiana, who sets out on the same pilgrimage, accompanied by her neighbor Mercy, despite the objections of Mrs. Timorous and others.

The work, remarkable for the beauty and simplicity of its language, the vividness of its characterization, and the author's sense of humor and feeling for the world of nature, was circulated at first primarily in uneducated circles. Universal in its appeal, it has been translated into well over one hundred languages.

Included in *Pilgrim's Progress* are numerous poems reflecting upon the prose narrative. The poem which became our hymn appeared first in the 1684 edition. It follows and reinforces Valiant-for-Truth's account of his parents and friends who tried to discourage his being a pilgrim:

> Who would true Valour See,
> Let him come hither;
> One here will Constant be,
> Come Wind, come Weather.
> There's no Discouragement,
> Shall make him once Relent,
> His first avow'd Intent,
> To be a Pilgrim.
>
> Who so beset him round
> With dismal Storys,
> Do but themselves confound;
> His strength the more is,
> No Lyon can him fright,
> He'll with a Gyant Fight,
> But he will have a right,
> To be a Pilgrim.

Hobgoblin, nor foul Fiend,
Can daunt his Spirit:
He knows, he at the end,
Shall Life Inherit.
Then Fancies fly away,
He'll fear not what men say,
He'll labor Night and Day,
To be a Pilgrim.[92]

Percy Dearmer writes:

In 1904, we who were working at the *English Hymnal* felt that some cheerful and manly hymns must be added to the usual repertory; and this song sprang to my mind. It was a daring thing to add the song to a hymnbook, and it had never been attempted before. To include the hobgoblins would have been to ensure disaster; to ask the congregation of St. Ignotus, Erewhon Park, to invite all to come and look at them, if they wished to see true valor would have been difficult. But when, with the help of the marvelous folk-tune which Vaughan Williams had discovered, we had made a great hymn, it became easy for our imitators to complain that we had altered the words. We felt that we had done rightly; and that no one would have been more distressed than Bunyan himself to have people singing about hobgoblins in church. He had not written it for a hymn, and it was not suitable as a hymn without adaptation.[93]

Bunyan's text was set to music by Winfrid Douglas, while on the train between New York City and Peekskill, where he resided on the grounds of the Community of St. Mary in a stone house named "St. Dunstan's Cottage."

∞

H.R. Haweis, in his foreword to an 1898 edition of *The Pilgrim's Progress*, suggests that Bunyan's great work

> ... did for Protestantism what Dante did for Roman Catholicism—whilst exposing sometimes naively its weak points, it affirmed its doctrines, and popularized their application to current life. ... Bunyan supplied that imaginative touch and that glow of pictorial sentiment without which no religious message seems to win the masses.[94]

Like Jesus, who did not teach the people "without a parable" (Mt.13:32), both Bunyan and Dante were able to capture the essence of religion through a rousing good story. John Dominic Crossan's fascinating book *In Parables* includes some comments about why such stories wield their power. He quotes Ezra Pound:

> In writing poems, the author must use his *image* because he sees it or feels it, *not* because he thinks he can use it to back up some creed. All poetic language is the language of exploration. ... The image is itself the speech. The image is the word beyond formulated language.[95]

In Bunyan's tale, as in Dante's *Commedia* and the parables of Jesus, the story can stand on its own. We do not need to interpret it in order to enjoy it.

Nevertheless, the story works on us, usually unnoticed, at an unconscious level. The fact is that the narratives we read—

or, in this day, watch—begin to shape the way we think about the world. Recently, a six-year-old boy shot and killed a classmate because the stories he imbibed from violent television programs shaped the way he thought, before he was old enough to understand the consequences of violence in "real life."

When I was in elementary school, my favorite book was Louisa May Alcott's *Little Women*, the story of the close-knit March family, written in the mid-nineteenth century. I used to read and re-read it, each time trying to decide which of the four sisters—Meg, Jo, Beth, or Amy—I liked best. Because I lived and breathed that story so often, the story began to shape me. Imagine my surprise when I opened my yellowed childhood copy to discover the Preface:

> Go then, my little Book, and show to all
> That entertain and bid thee welcome shall,
> What thou dost keep close shut up in thy breast;
> And wish what thou dost show them to be blest
> To them for good, may make them choose to be
> Pilgrims better, by far, than thee or me.
> Tell them of Mercy; she is one
> Who early hath her pilgrimage begun.
> Yet, let young damsels learn of her to prize
> The world which is to come, and so be wise;
> For little tripping maids may follow God
> Along the ways which saintly feet have trod.
> Adapted from JOHN BUNYAN[96]

John Bunyan himself knew the power of narrative to inspire or dishearten us. One of the dangers that his pilgrim Christian encountered was the encounter with those "who so beset him round / with dismal stories." That obstacle to the journey was overcome only by Christian's vow "to be a pilgrim."

What stories have shaped each of us through life? In my own, *Little Women* soon had companions: Dante, the Bible, and biographies of people I admire. These narratives, which have almost become a part of my nervous system, inspire and encourage me. They remind me that my own life is a narrative in the making, and that my path, perhaps, might someday influence others. They help me to labor, night and day, to be a pilgrim.

Independence Day   *July 4*

Hymn 591   O God of earth and altar
Gilbert Keith Chesterton (1874–1936)

G. K. Chesterton was born in Kensington and educated at St. Paul's School, London, where he won the Milton Prize for English poetry. After studying at the Slade School of Art, he began his career as a writer of art criticism for the *Spectator* and other periodicals. From this field, he branched out into a wide range of topics and became "one of the most vivacious, versatile and provocative figures" in the field of journalism.[97] He produced penetrating literary appraisals of Browning, Dickens, and Swinburne. A militant foe of almost everything modern, he condemned the whole economic system of both Socialism and industrial capitalism and attacked much of contemporary religious thought.

He surprised everyone by his conversion to Roman Catholicism in 1922, after he had come under the influence of the Frenchman Hilaire Belloc. He was convinced that the Middle Ages were history's golden age and that the cure for the social ills of an industrial society was a return to the medieval guild system. He insisted that the means of destroying Puritanism and bringing back "merrie England" was a return to the Roman Catholic Church.

It has been said that few men during the first half of the twentieth century aroused more diverse reactions. While some regarded him as an intolerant medievalist, George Bernard Shaw, among others, called him a colossal genius.

His energy was prodigious; he was able to dictate 13,000 to 14,000 words a week while maintaining a busy lecture schedule as well. He wrote some one hundred stories, novels, plays, biographies, and volumes of verse during his lifetime. He is best known in the United States for his series of *Father Brown* detective stories.

"O God of earth and altar," written in 1906, is Chesterton's response to the self-satisfied mood and materialistic and morally lax lifestyle in England at the beginning of the twentieth century. Specifically, Chesterton was outraged by the Boer War, to which he was bitterly opposed. The text reverberates with the intensity of an Old Testament prophecy. The poet uses vivid language to indict rulers whose duplicity and "easy speeches" give comfort to "cruel men."

In stanza three, the poet reveals his characteristic enthusiasm for the Middle Ages, referring to the "three estates" of medieval society, "prince and priest and thrall."

The text was first printed in the monthly magazine *The Commonwealth*. It was given to Percy Dearmer and included in the *English Hymnal* set to an English folk song arranged by Vaughan Williams.

☙

This strong hymn is, unfortunately, never out of date. On the cover of *The New Yorker* magazine which arrived during Holy Week in 2000 was a cartoon which at first glance looks like three men, smiling manically, harvesting the fruit of an apple tree. On closer examination, these are very strange apples: dollar bills!

As I turn the pages, I encounter advertisements: "The thrill of a sport sedan. The serenity of a luxury sedan. Capabilities beyond any sedan." "Opulent Accommodations." "The first half million is the hardest." "At your service. Whether it's pronounced *en su servicio*, or *al vostro servizio*, we will tend to your every desire."

And yet children go to bed hungry in the richest nation in the world. Many in this country have no access to health care. The discrepancy between rich and poor widens. Columnist Donella Meadows writes, "This is an economy of illusion. It is a mean economy, as worker salaries stagnate, worker benefits plummet, CEO compensation soars and the rich extract interest from the poor and throw tax burdens onto the middle class. It is a financially unstable economy in a socially unstable society."[98]

There is no doubt that walls of gold can entomb us. Yet public policy and private enterprise too often are based on an economics that benefits the rich rather than on more permanent values, such as justice, health, equity, and stewardship of the earth's resources. Easy speeches and "lies of tongue and pen" propagate the assumption that those who are wealthy deserve to get richer and those who are poor must have lacked the initiative or intelligence to accumulate wealth and therefore do not deserve it.

The church needs to be countercultural and hold out an alternative route to happiness. We are, in fact, tied "in a living tether" with everyone else on earth: princes, priests, thralls, starving children in Mozambique, homeless mothers in our nation's slums, and destitute widows in the former Soviet Union. When greed becomes a way of life, the walls of gold isolate us from the rest of humanity. These walls can never protect us from the truth: this is not the way God intends us to live.

Proper 9: The Sunday closest to July 6

Hymn 522,523   Glorious things of thee are spoken
*John Newton (1725–1807)**

For much of his life, John Newton wrote a hymn each week which explored the biblical themes of his Sunday sermon. It is likely that "Glorious things of thee are spoken" shared its origins with a sermon Newton preached sometime before February 1779, on Isaiah 33:20–21:

> Look on Zion, the city of our appointed festivals!
> Your eyes will see Jerusalem,
> a quiet habitation, an immovable tent,
> whose stakes will never be pulled up,
> and none of whose ropes will be broken.
>
> But there the Lord in majesty will be for us
> a place of broad rivers and streams,
> where no galley with oars can go,
> nor stately ship can pass.

------

*For additional biographical information, see 55–58.

The hymn first appeared in print in Newton's *Olney Hymns* in 1779, with five stanzas. In *The Hymnal 1982* the final stanza has been omitted, possibly because of the subtle reference to the Calvinist doctrine of election:

> Saviour, if of Zion's city
>   I, thro' grace a member am;
> Let the world deride or pity,
>   I will glory in thy name:
> Fading is the world's pleasure,
>   All his boasted pomp and show;
> Solid joys and lasting treasure,
>   None but Zion's children know.[99]

The first tune was composed by Haydn as the Austrian national anthem. The second tune was written in 1941 to replace the original tune because of its association with the Nazi regime. The composer was head of religious broadcasts at the wartime BBC headquarters in Bristol.

 లు

We all long for the perfect community in which to make our home. Early in the last century, many young people left the rural environment in which they had grown up for the excitement of big city life. In the middle of the century, new parents, including my own, left deteriorating cities for the suburbs, seeking utopia in the form of green space, fresh air, and good schools. When the suburbs became congested with strip malls and traffic, the prosperous moved to "exurbia," sometimes returning to the same rural land vacated a century before by youth seeking the thrills of city life.

What is the perfect place in which to live? The Disney Corporation tried to create it in "Celebration," a planned town near Orlando, Florida. Celebration has neat houses with front porches, manicured lawns, and lots of rules. People who moved there hoped they were moving to Eden. But it was not long before the inevitable conflicts about government or education or architecture began to disrupt the longed-for harmony.

When the Israelites of Isaiah's time thought of the perfect community, their eyes turned toward Jerusalem. Especially after their homeland had been invaded by the strong powers across their borders, they longed for the time when the holy city would once again be a secure place. This would happen when a messianic king would reign and their enemies would flee: "No longer will you see the insolent people, the people of an obscure speech that you cannot comprehend, stammering in a language that you cannot understand." (Is.33:19)

John Newton has taken the image of the messianic Jerusalem, or "Zion," and baptized it. The model community is no longer on this earth: it is in heaven, the new Jerusalem, and the Messiah is there already. It is a gated community: only the redeemed are permitted entry. The inhabitants are cared for by God, who sends the cloud and the fire of the Exodus story to remind them of the divine presence. A stream of living water assuages their thirst, and they are fed by holy manna.

While I prefer to live in a more diverse neighborhood than John Newton's, I suppose that he has the right idea. On this earth, no perfect village, town, or city exists. That is because true community is not a place; it is a gathering of interconnected human beings. When the controversies and problems of the places where we dwell overwhelm us, it is tempting to either move away or to give up, and look forward to dwelling someday in the heavenly Jerusalem.

But I think that God would want us instead to become

"blest inhabitants" of our earthly cities, suburbs, or rural towns, by finding the motivation and strength to make our communities more like our vision of Zion. We need not become kings or priests. We can merely become involved citizens, learning to work together, remembering that our neighbors are all God's sons and daughters, even those who are "people of an obscure speech that you cannot comprehend, stammering in a language that you cannot understand."

God surely wants to abide not merely in the heavenly Jerusalem, but wherever we live now, on earth, helping us in urban—or suburban, or rural—renewal, transforming these places into havens of security and peace.

Proper 10: *The Sunday closest to July 13*

Hymn 590   O Jesus Christ, may grateful hymns be rising
Bradford Gray Webster (1898–1991)

Bradford Gray Webster was born in Syracuse, New York, and educated at Amherst College, the Boston School of Theology, and Garrett Theological Seminary. He was minister in the Central New York Conference of the Methodist Church for ten years, and in the Old Geneseo Conference for thirty years, serving churches in Gowanda, Syracuse, and Buffalo until his retirement in 1964.

He was active since childhood in the Boy Scouts of America and throughout his life was involved in a number of civic organizations, including councils of churches, ministerial associations, and community organizations. A collection of his poems was published under the title *Songs in the Night*.

"O Jesus Christ, may grateful hymns be rising" was the Hymn Society of America's first choice among the hymns submitted for the Convocation on Urban Life in America, called by the Council of Bishops of the Methodist Church. It was published in *Five New Hymns for the City*, published by the Hymn Society and sung at the convocation in Columbus, Ohio, in February 1954. Since that time it has been included in many hymnals in the United States.

It is matched in *The Hymnal 1982* with a strong English tune composed in the first part of the twentieth century.

℘

Before we moved to a college town in rural Ohio, I commuted by train from the suburbs into New York City and took the Lexington Avenue subway downtown to Wall Street. There, amidst the canyons of the financial district, stood Trinity Church, its spire bravely challenging its enormous neighbors.

At one time in New York's history, it had been a landmark for sailors seeking the harbor. In modern times, it has been dwarfed—but only architecturally. It was quite clear when I worked there that, even when compared with the power embodied in the banking and investment business seething around it, Trinity was a place of enormous strength.

The worship within the neo-Gothic building inspired and invigorated parishioners and staff to venture and to dare in many ways, such as serving the homeless through creating a shelter in the balcony of historic St. Paul's Chapel, or building a retirement community for seniors on nearby Fulton Street. A series of noonday concerts attracted men and women aching for a respite from the frenzy of the stock market. A weekly healing service attracted the sick in body and spirit. The quiet church was constantly used by people, from professionals to the jobless, praying and resting.

Trinity, of course, continues in these ministries. It is but one of the many city churches that respond to the needs of the urban community; I have chosen it as an illustration because I know it best. As governmental agencies withdraw from service to the most neglected members of society, city churches have become places of sacrificial courage in their service to the fallen, the stumbling, and the lonely.

But their function as places of beauty and worship has become not less, but more important, as the extent of their ministry to those outside their walls has grown. Like the great cathedrals of England, the churches of our cities are embodiments of a point of view that is markedly different from the bustling city life around them. Instead of celebrating the wizards of the corporate world, they celebrate a Lord who took the form of a servant. Instead of prizing busy-ness and utility, they make an effort to become oases of peace, places where the human soul can be fed through music, liturgy, architecture, and silence.

What better prayer for these churches than this hymn—"Show us your Spirit, brooding o'er each city"—imploring God to enable us to be signs and bearers of divine healing, pity, and love.

Proper 11: *The Sunday closest to July 20*

Hymn 487   Come, my Way, my Truth, my Life
George Herbert (1593–1633)*

"Come, my Way, my Truth, my Life" first appeared in *The Temple*, the posthumous collection of Herbert's poems, published in Cambridge in 1633.

Carl P. Daw, Jr. comments that, like much of Herbert's poetry, "the text derives a considerable part of its energy from the strict structure into which its allusive phrases have been fitted. Like springs compressed into a box, paradoxes are packed into ordered lines that belie their complexity."[100]

Stanza one alludes to John 14:6 ("Jesus said to him, 'I am the way, and the truth, and the life'"), reiterating the three elements of the opening line and expanding each with the formula: "such a ___ as." The way is "such a way that gives us breath": it is a path that leaves us not breathless but refreshed. The truth is "such a truth as ends all strife": it sets us free (as in Jn.8:32) and leads to harmony rather than to quarrels. The final phrase affirms Christ's victory over death.

In the second stanza, Herbert refers to Jesus as Light, Feast, and Strength. Jesus is the "light of the world" (Jn.8:12), the "bread that came down from heaven" (Jn.6:41), the "power ...dwelling within" (2 Cor:12:9). His light shines before the world and reveals God's bounty: "No one after lighting a lamp puts it in a cellar, but on the lampstand so that those

---

*For additional biographical background, see *Awake, My Soul!*, 194–197 and 229-232.

who enter may see the light." (Lk. 11:33). Our experience of Christ's presence in the eucharistic banquet becomes richer with our reenactment of the mystery over time. Carl Daw suggests that the image "such a feast as mends in length" may allude to the wedding feast at Cana, where the best wine came at the end of the feast. (Jn. 2:10)[101]

The final stanza may take its inspiration from 1 Corinthians 13, with its emphasis on abiding love from which we as creatures can never be separated. The final phrase includes all three epithets from the first, transforming the noun "joy" into the verb "joys." As Daw writes, "[T]hus the threefold structure of the three stanzas, 'a trinity of trinities,' comes to a comprehensive and emphatic conclusion."[102]

This text was set to music by Ralph Vaughan Williams in his *Five Mystical Songs*. "Come, my Way, my Truth, my Life" is an arrangement of that composition.

⁓

Lord, how can man preach thy eternal word?
 He is a brittle crazy glass:
Yet in thy temple thou dost him afford
 This glorious and transcendent place,
 To be a window, through thy grace.[103]

In the back of George Herbert's little church in Bemerton near Salisbury is a window that is a portrait in stained glass of the poet. Light shines through it in the late afternoon, just as it shone through Herbert's poetry and through his ministry as a gentle and devoted country parson.

The light of God certainly shines through the exquisite "Come, my Way, my Truth, my life." In his introduction to a volume of Herbert's writings, A.M. Alchin points out that Herbert

. . . uses the Bible as a source for a living language with which to talk about the encounter between God and the reader, or with which to describe his own experiences of God in his own life. . . . When Herbert does this, he is making the claim that the Bible is not a closed narrative, but an account of a story that is still going on.[104]

The words of Jesus in the Gospels became part of the narrative of Herbert's life. He lived them in his ministry, wove them into his poetry, and explored them through his prayer. He would surely ask us, also, to let these words become transparent through our experience of them.

How is Jesus our Way, our Truth, our Life, our Light, our Feast, and our Strength? We would do well to ponder this question and then to write our own versions of the answers. It is unlikely that we would be as poetic as Herbert, but this exercise would demonstrate to us that the Bible "is not a closed narrative, but an account of a story that is still going on."

We might discover, with Herbert, that Jesus is the Way because our relationship with him "gives us breath," moderating the frenetic pace of modern life. We might find that, when we are blinded by anger and fear, the Truth of Jesus' witness that all human beings are loved by God will open our eyes. Jesus' Light may shine on the world we take for granted, so that we discover that the life God gives us is indeed a feast.

Each one of Herbert's phrases could provide sustenance for a lifetime of prayer. Each of us will see them through the prism of our own experience. Through this poetry, God's light shines through the "brittle crazy glass" of our lives, and begins to transform our hearts so that, like Herbert's, they are radiant with joy and love.

Proper 12: The Sunday closest to July 27

Hymn 411   O bless the Lord, my soul!
James Montgomery (1771–1854)

James Montgomery, the son of a Moravian minister, was born in Irvine, Ayrshire, England, and brought up in a religious atmosphere. When he was six years old, his parents sailed as missionaries to the West Indies, and he went to live at a boys' boarding school run by some Moravian Brethren at Fulneck in Yorkshire. Here, according to Montgomery, "whatever we did was done in the name and for the sake of Jesus Christ, whom we were taught to regard in the amiable and endearing light of a friend and brother."[105] An illustration of this attitude is the prayer of one of the boys after a change in the menu:

> O Lord, bless us little children and make us very good.
> We thank thee for what we have received. Oh, bless
> this good chocolate and give us more of it.[106]

Stimulated by the heritage of Moravian hymns he heard at school, Montgomery began to write poetry at the age of ten. Unfortunately, his preoccupation with writing poetry caused him to be dismissed at the age of fourteen, and he was sent to work in a bakeshop. He ran away at sixteen, with only a few coins and some specimens of his verse in his pocket. He became a clerk in a bookshop in London, and, in response to a want ad, traveled to Sheffield, where he became assistant to the editor and owner of the *Sheffield Register*, a radical newspaper. When the owner of the paper fled the country to avoid political prosecution, Montgomery took over the paper, renamed it *The Sheffield Iris*, and continued to edit it for thirty-one years.

The French Revolution was in progress, and the population of Sheffield supported the revolutionaries; Montgomery printed a song celebrating the fall of the Bastille and was imprisoned in York Castle. Soon after his release, he printed a tirade against the way the military commander had put down a riot in the town and he was imprisoned again. He spent his time in prison writing poetry.

He was a well-known public figure in Sheffield, who spoke out against the slave trade, child labor, state lotteries, and in support of foreign missions and the Bible Society. He was an ecumenist before his time, joining in public worship with Anglicans, Independents, Baptists, and Methodists, and cooperating with the outlawed Roman Catholics, Unitarians, and Quakers in local charitable endeavors.

Montgomery wrote over four hundred hymns, of which more than a hundred are still in use. Many of them appeared in Cotterill's *Selections of Psalms and Hymns for Public and Private Use, adapted to the Festivals of the Church of England* (1819), as well as in his own collections: *Songs of Zion* (1822), *The Christian Psalmist* (1825), and *Original Hymns for Public, Private and Social Devotion* (1853). His *Poetical Works* appeared in several editions.

Montgomery integrated his championship of human rights with his gift of poetry in both his life and his vocation. The hymnologist Julian writes:

> With the faith of a strong man he united the beauty and simplicity of a child. Richly poetic without exuberance, dogmatic without uncharitableness, tender without

sentimentality, elaborate without diffusiveness, richly musical without apparent effort, he has bequeathed to the Church of Christ wealth which could only have come from a true genius and a sanctified heart.[107]

"O bless the Lord, my soul," a paraphrase of Psalm 103:1–5 and 8, appeared in the eighth edition of Cotterill's *Selection of Psalms and Hymns*. It draws heavily on phrases of Coverdale's translation of the psalm found in editions of the Book of Common Prayer prior to 1979.

It is matched with a eighteenth-century tune which reflects the joy and confidence of the text.

༺

"O bless the Lord, my soul!" This gentle text illustrates what an influence teachers and parents can have upon our children's image of God.

Montgomery remembered from his years at the Moravian boarding school that "we were taught to regard [Jesus] in the amiable and endearing light of a friend and brother." As an adult paraphrasing the irenic Psalm 103, Montgomery adds his own blessings: "He clothes thee with his love, / upholds thee with his truth." He never outgrew his belief in a beneficent God.

One of the most luminous books I know about children and their faith is Sofia Cavalletti's *The Religious Potential of the Child: The Description of an Experience with Children from Ages Three to Six*,[108] in which she describes her approach to the religious education of young children. Her method, called "the catechesis of the Good Shepherd," which she began exploring in the 1950s, was influenced by the work of Maria Montessori and, in turn, has influenced Christian educators like Jerome Berryman and Sonja Stewart.

Cavalletti believes that the goal of Christian education is to help children to respond to God's immeasurable love:

> The child needs an infinite, global love, such as no human being is able to give him. No child, I believe, has ever been loved to the degree that he wanted and needed. For the child, love is more necessary than food. . . . In the contact with God the child finds the nourishment his being requires, nourishment the child needs in order to grow in harmony.[109]

Those who are blessed with the care and teaching of children can attest to the fact that, in turn, they teach us, and we can bless the fact that their need for love reminds us of our own.

Proper 13: The Sunday closest to August 3

Hymn 420   When in our music God is glorified
F. Pratt Green (b. 1903)

Fred Pratt Green, the son of a successful businessman who was also a Wesleyan Methodist local preacher, was born near Liverpool, England, in 1903. He was educated at Huyton High School, Wallasey Grammar School, Rydal School, and Didsbury College in Manchester. A sermon on John Masefield's *The Everlasting Mercy* was the catalyst for his call to the Wesleyan Methodist ministry, and he was ordained in 1928.

During his years of active circuit ministry in the north and south of England, he wrote plays and a few hymns, as well as two collections of poems: *This Unlikely Earth* (1952), *The Skating Parson* (1963).

After his retirement, he assembled a third collection, *The Old Couple* (1976), and wrote about three hundred hymns and Christian songs. Green has been credited with starting the "hymn explosion" that occurred in England in the latter part of the twentieth century. His poems also appeared in many periodicals, including *The New Yorker*.

In 1982, Emory University, Atlanta, conferred upon the poet an honorary doctorate in Humane Letters, and the Hymn Society of America named him a fellow. Much of his work is now collected in *The Hymns and Ballads of Fred Pratt Green* (1982) and *Later Hymns and Ballads and Fifty Poems* (1989).

"When in our music God is glorified" was written in 1972 at the request of John Wilson, who wanted new words for Stanford's festive tune ENGLEBERG. The text appeared on the front cover of the Hymn Society of America's journal *The Hymn* in the summer of 1973. The poem is based loosely on Psalm 150, Mark 14:26 and Matthew 26:30 ("When they had sung the hymn, they went out to the Mount of Olives").

❧

For ten years, my husband and I have traveled to England to attend the Southern Cathedrals Festival, a joint offering of the choirs of Salisbury, Winchester, and Chichester cathedrals. It is a feast for the soul to hear great music in those holy spaces. Afterwards, I always feel as if I have attended a long silent retreat: at peace, in harmony, and in touch with God.

Judging from the attendance at this event, I am not alone in finding that music touches a great chord within my soul. The music of the Christian tradition, from plainsong to Bach to Britten and beyond, not only celebrates the faith we have shared throughout the centuries: it deepens that faith.

In the concert hall as well as the cathedral, music speaks to me as the language of God. The Swiss Protestant theologian Karl Barth wrote that "if I ever get to heaven, I would first of all seek out Mozart and only then inquire after Augustine, St. Thomas, Luther, Calvin, and Schleiermacher."[110] In a "Letter of Thanks to Mozart," he tells the composer that "Whenever I listen to you, I am transported to the threshold of a world which in sunlight and storm, by day and by night, is a good and ordered world. . . . With an ear open to your musical dialectic, one can be young and become old, and work and rest, be content and sad: in short, one can live."[111]

In *The Magician's Nephew*, the sixth book of C.S. Lewis's *Chronicles of Narnia*, the boy Digory is given a vision of the creation of the world:

> In the darkness something was happening at last. A voice had begun to sing. . . . There were no words. There was hardly even a tune. But it was, beyond comparison, the most beautiful noise he had ever heard. . . . [Then] the blackness overhead, all at once, was blazing with stars. . . . The Voice rose and rose, till all the air was shaking with it. And just as it swelled to the mightiest and most glorious sound it had yet produced, the sun rose. . . . And as its beams shot across the land the travellers could see for the first time what sort of place they were in. It was a valley through which a broad, swift river wound its way, flowing eastward towards the sun. Southward there were mountains, northward there were lower hills. . . . They made you feel excited; until you saw the Singer himself, and then you forgot everything else.[112]

When I let myself just be still in the presence of music, I enter the presence of the Singer who was at the beginning of time. The music, whether I am listening to an effervescent Mozart concerto or practicing a Bach fugue on the piano, resolves my own dissonances and creates a harmony and order that were not there before. It "tunes" me, by drawing me deep into myself, and thus beyond myself, toward a more profound "Alleluia!"

Proper 14: The Sunday closest to *August 10*

Hymn 369   How wondrous great, how glorious bright
Isaac Watts (1674–1748)*; st. 3 *Caryl Micklem (b.1925)*

It is interesting to note that, even seventy years after the publication of this hymn in 1707, there were still Christians who believed that no hymns other than metrical psalms were proper for worship. An incident in Elizabeth, New Jersey, in May 1780, during the American Revolution is proof. George Washington's militia ran out of wadding for their guns, and the local Presbyterian pastor, obviously of the "metrical hymn school," used the opportunity to bring out batches of Watts's hymns, shouting "Give 'em Watts, boys; give 'em Watts!"

Nine years later, during the first General Assembly of the Presbyterian Church in Philadelphia, a clergyman rode on horseback from his Kentucky parish to plead with the assembly to refuse to allow the pernicious error of adopting the use

---

*For additional biographical information, see *A Closer Walk*, 27, 233–234 and *Awake, My Soul!*, 54–57, 185–186.

of Watts's hymns in public worship; the assembly, however, requested him to use Christian charity toward those who differed from him in their views. One wonders what these early dissidents would think of the inclusion of eleven of Watts's hymn texts in the 1990 Presbyterian hymnal, to say nothing of sixteen texts in *The Hymnal 1982*!

Carlyl Micklem, who contributed to the third stanza of this Watts hymn, is an English Congregational minister, an active hymnwriter of both texts and tunes, and has been chairman of the Hymn Society of Great Britain and Ireland.

The text is matched with a new tune written especially for use with it by an American hymnwriter.

❧

I wonder if Isaac Watts had ever read Dante's vision of heaven in his *Commedia*, or *Divine Comedy*. Certainly his picture of the Creator who "dwells amidst the dazzling light of vast eternity" would have been recognized by that medieval poet.

Like Watts, Dante knows that "our soaring spirits upward rise / to reach the burning throne": we long to see God because of an innate longing. The narrator of the *Commedia* is told, on his pilgrimage through Paradise, "your life the Supreme Beneficence breathes forth immediately, and He so enamours it of Himself that it desires Him ever after."[113]

When Dante finally reaches the end of his journey, he sees the vision of a great white rose consisting of the souls of the redeemed. In the center of the rose there was a light in which were three circles, one "reflected by the other as rainbow by rainbow, and the third seemed fire breathed forth equally from the one and the other."[114] As he gazed on it, he saw that one of the circles was

. . . painted with our likeness, for which my sight was wholly given to it. . . . As the geometer who sets all his mind to the squaring of the circle and for all his thinking does not discover the principle he needs, such was I at that strange sight. I wished to see how the image was fitted to the circle and how it had its place there; but my own wings were not sufficient for that, had not my mind been smitten by a flash wherein came its wish. Here power failed the high phantasy; but now my desire and will, like a wheel that spins with even motion, were revolved by the Love that moves the sun and the other stars.[115]

Watts's reason "stretched its wings" as well, to imagine the vision of the blessed Three in the Almighty One, but his wings were, like Dante's, insufficient.

Both poets become speechless at the mystery of the Trinity dwelling in vast eternity. But both also remind us of the response of the human being to even imagining such a vision. We respond through worship: "let faith in humble notes adore / the great mysterious King."

And we respond through our lives. Once we have glimpsed, if only in our imaginations, the Love that moves the sun and the other stars, we know that what we really want is what God wants: that our "desire and will" be "revolved" by that Love.

This view of heaven is no escape from terrestrial life. It is, instead, the catalyst for a life lived in loving service to others. In awakening our longing for the vision of God, it energizes us for today's duties and challenges. It also reassures us with the hope that, at the end of all our todays, lies a dazzling vision of Love.

Proper 15: *The Sunday closest to* *August 17*

Hymn 324   Let all mortal flesh keep silence
Liturgy of St. James; para. *Gerard Moultrie (1829–1885)*

The Liturgy of St. James is an ancient liturgy, existing in both a Greek and Syrian form. It is traditionally ascribed to James, the brother of Jesus and the first Bishop of Jerusalem. The liturgy became traditional in the Syriac-, Armenian-, and Georgian-speaking part of the church. In certain Orthodox churches, it is still used on October 23, the day the Eastern church commemorates St. James's death, as well as on the Sunday after Christmas.

In the fifth-century form of the Liturgy of St. James, this "Cherubic Hymn" was used at the presentation of the sacred elements at the time of the offertory. It was later adopted for inclusion in the Liturgy of St. Basil, the standard liturgy of Greek Orthodoxy, for use on Easter Eve.

The metrical translation was composed by Gerard Moultrie for the second edition of *Lyra Eucharistica*. Born in Rugby, England, the son of the rector of Rugby parish, Moultrie was educated at Rugby School and at Exeter College, Oxford. He held various chaplaincies and spent most of his life as vicar of Southleigh and warden of St. James' College, Southleigh. He wrote much religious verse and many hymns, both original compositions and translations from Greek, Latin, and German.

The text was matched with a seventeenth-century French carol arranged by Ralph Vaughan Williams, one of the editors of the *English Hymnal*.   ⁓

I will never forget my first silent retreat. In my final year before college, I went to visit a convent in Catonsville, Maryland, where a high school friend of mine had been raised by the sisters in the adjoining children's home which they tended. Entering the convent grounds was like stepping into a great ocean of peace. The sisters habitually went about their work quietly, and the "Great Silence" spanned the night from after Compline, the final evening office, to after breakfast.

During the day or so I was on retreat, I did not speak at all. I felt myself relaxing into the silence like a swimmer floating in salt water. It was as if the silence supported and surrounded me as I plunged into the ocean that was God.

Silence is still necessary for my journey. Our home is a quiet one, although it was not always so when our children were young. Since my husband and I both take a while to become alert in the morning, we do not talk much over the breakfast table. At some time during the day, I need time alone in my study, to pray, to reflect, and to write, and the day does not go well if I have missed this time.

I do not think that I am unique in needing times when my "mortal flesh keeps silence." Certainly, the great masters of prayer have taught the necessity for silence. This, of course, is the essence of contemplative prayer: to be still in the presence of God.

While some people are more adept at praying with words, even in verbal prayer there is the need to stop every once in a while to listen, as well. Even in the prayer in which we ponder a passage of Scripture, there are times when we need to pause and sit quietly, so that the words and images can reverberate within us and God can speak to us through them.

Outward silence is merely a sign of the silence that we can carry within us. The movement of "Hesychasm" in the Eastern Orthodox church, the origins of which extend back to the fourth and fifth centuries, teaches that silence and peace can be our constant companions, no matter how busy our lives.

We discover this silence when we discover that the Source of our being can be found within us. Hesychasm teaches its disciples to find it through the continual reciting of a prayer to Jesus. But there are many other ways to "Be still and know that I am God." (Ps. 46:11) We can be attentive to our breathing, both when we are at prayer and when we go about our lives, remembering that God is the source of our life. We can take time for a quiet walk in the woods or the park. We can, paradoxically, listen to music, not as background but as a focus of our attention.

Silence not only gives our souls an opportunity to expand and breathe. It also is our best—and sometimes only—response to the mystery of God.

This is true both in our personal prayer and in our worship, when observing periods of silence helps us join the ranks of the host of heaven in praising the God for whom we will never have adequate words.

Proper 16: The Sunday closest to *August 24*

Hymn 687,688   A mighty fortress is our God
Martin Luther (1483–1546)*; tr. *Frederic Henry Hedge (1805–1890)*

Eine Feste Burg ("A mighty fortress is our God") ranks among the most important of all Christian hymns. It is one of the earliest examples of the genre of psalm paraphrase.

Its text was called by the poet Heine "the *Marseillaise* of the Reformation";[116] others called it "God Almighty's Grenadier March" or "The Battle Hymn of the Reformation."[117] This view of the hymn's purpose was given musical reinforcement by such composers as Mendelssohn in his *Reformation Symphony*, Meyerbeer in his opera *Les Hugenotten*, and Wagner in his *Kaisersmarsch*.

This interpretation, however, runs counter to Luther's understanding of his own hymn, which he entitled "A Hymn of Comfort." He envisioned it as an expression of the reasons for Christian hope in times of trial and conflict, not as a vehicle of belligerent Protestantism.

Luther is known to have found comfort in Psalm 46, on which this hymn is based. He himself wrote a brief outline of the psalm, which parallels his hymnic form of the text:

> This is a psalm of thanksgiving which the people of Israel sang at that time in response to the miracles of God, who had defended and sustained the city of

---

*For additional biographical information, see *A Closer Walk*, 83–85 and *New Every Morning*, 24–28, 43–44.

Jerusalem, where they lived, against the rantings and ravings of all kings and nations, and preserved it in peace against all war and conflict. Then, speaking after the manner of scripture, the essence of the city is portrayed as a little spring, a small rivulet, that will not run dry, in contrast to the great rivers and oceans of the nations (that is, the great kingdoms, principalities and estates) that will dry up and disappear.

But we sing in praise to God because he is with us— God who miraculously preserves his Word and Christendom against the gates of hell, against the ravings of all devils, fanatical spirits, the world, the flesh, sin, death, etc., so that our little spring remains a living fountain, while foul and stinking drains, puddles and cisterns will run dry.[118]

Luther never drew a strong line of distinction between the hardships of life and the internal struggles of the soul. The hymn was written sometime around 1527–1528, and causes for anxiety were plentiful. In 1527, Wittenberg was experiencing an outbreak of the plague, and a report had been received that a man named Leonard Kaiser had been martyred for confessing the evangelical faith. It was the tenth anniversary of the posting of the 95 Theses, and Luther's wife was pregnant with their second child.

Luther interprets Psalm 46 in strongly Christological terms, anticipating Isaac Watts by almost two centuries. He pictures the strife between life and death as the struggle between Christ and the devil. Robin Leaver writes that the key to the whole hymn may be found in the final line of the final stanza: "his kingdom is for ever."[119] Toward the end of 1528, Luther was also working on his catechetical exposition of the Lord's Prayer, and he wrote the following about "Thy kingdom come":

> What is the kingdom of God? Answer: Simply what we learned in the Creed, namely, that God sent his Son, Christ our Lord, into the world to redeem and deliver us from the power of the devil and to bring us to himself and rule as a king of righteousness, life, and salvation against sin, death, and an evil conscience. . . . So we pray that, led by the Holy Spirit, many may come into the kingdom of grace and become partakers of salvation, so that we may all remain together eternally in this kingdom which has now made its appearance among us.[120]

Within Luther's own lifetime, *Ein feste Burg* was translated into many European languages, including one by Miles Coverdale (see pages 217–218) in his *Goostly psalmes and spirituall songes* in 1535. Almost five centuries later, the hymn is sung in at least two hundred different languages, and there are about one hundred different English translations, each one an attempt at the difficult task of presenting Luther's rugged poetry in the form of English verse.

The translation by Frederick H. Hedge, a Unitarian minister, which first appeared in 1852, is the one used predominantly in North American hymnals. Born in Cambridge, Massachusetts, Hedge was sent to study in Germany when he was thirteen years old, graduated from Harvard, studied theology, and was ordained in 1829. A pastor closely associated with the Transcendental Movement, he was also professor of both ecclesiastical history and of German at Harvard University.

The text is matched with two versions of Luther's tune: Luther's rhythmic form of the tune, and its later, more familiar form harmonized by Johann Sebastian Bach.

෧

I had never been inside a fortress like the ones Luther knew until we visited Salzburg a few years ago as part of a musical pilgrimage entitled "Tracing Mozart." Our quest took us on a funicular railway up the Mönchsberg, a hill overlooking the old town, to the Hohensalzburg, or "Salzburg castle," where we were to attend a concert. I had visited American colonial forts and Norman castles, but I have never seen such a fortification as this one. As we disembarked and walked the path to the entrance, high above us rose wall piled upon wall, all many feet thick. The mighty medieval and baroque edifice must have been, in its day, truly impervious to attack.

I think that the fondness for such enclosures is not merely a response to danger from outside, but the result of an innate sense of the comfort we feel when we find a safe space we call our own. I remember the delight of crawling into the snow fort my brothers and I built by our front door, the delicious world of the card table covered over with a bedsheet, the secret place under the forsythia bush in our back yard. These were places no adult body could enter; they were the fortifications of childhood.

The Hohensalzburg and its kindred enclosures, like our childhood secret places, keep out the rest of the world. Perhaps the closest equivalent today is the gated community, where those who can afford it can be protected from the dangers, real or imagined, lurking outside.

For Luther, God's presence was strength, solid as the walls of Salzburg's castle. He had experience of the presence of evil:

the world, "with devils filled," threatened to undo him. Protection from the outside, in the manner of a castle or card table, would not suffice against "the prince of darkness grim." Instead, the fortress needed to be within: the presence of Christ Jesus in his soul. Its weight grounded him in God's grace, its permanence reminded him of God's everlastingness.

Luther's fortress did not keep out the rest of the world. Instead, it protected him from the enemy within his own soul whose weapons were despair, cynicism, hatred, and fear. Because of the strength of his belief in God's grace, he had the courage to live and to write as God had called him to do. God's grace enabled him to remind others of God's presence and protection in their lives. This grace, stronger than any earthly castle, gives us the will to battle, on behalf of our world, against all that is not of God.

Proper 17: The Sunday closest to August 31

Hymn 644   How sweet the Name of Jesus sounds
John Newton (1725–1807)*

In *The History of the Church of England* by H.D. Wakeman, the author describes the English church at the time of the Evangelical Revival of the eighteenth century:

> The bishops were still amiable scholars, who lived in dignified ease apart from their clergy, attended the king's levee regularly, voted steadily for the party of the Minister who had appointed them, entertained the

---

*For additional biographical information, see 55–58.

country gentry when Parliament was not sitting, wrote learned books on points of classical scholarship, and were occasionally seen driving in state through the muddy country roads on their way to the chief towns of their diocese to hold confirmations. Of spiritual leadership they had little idea. Church patronage, which was mainly in the hands of the land-owning class, was largely used to make provision for life for the younger sons of the patrons.[121]

The hymnologist Albert Edward Bailey comments that "with such a spirit at the top of the hierarchy, precious little elixir of true religion could trickle down from above."[122] Instead, it sprang up from below through a "grass roots" religion like that of the Wesleys, Whitefield, and Newton, who enlisted his neighbor William Cowper in the task of writing hymns to express the simple, heartfelt religion he espoused.

An example of this religion is "How sweet the name of Jesus sounds." It was published in Book 1 of Newton's project, *Olney Hymns*, under the title "The name of Jesus." In this volume, the hymns are arranged in a biblical sequence, and the hymn appears as an exposition of a verse from the Song of Solomon: "Thy name is an as ointment poured forth." (Song 1:3)

In the fourth stanza, Newton speaks of "Jesus! my Shepherd, *Husband*, Friend," suggesting that the bride in the Song of Solomon stands for the individual soul. It has been suggested that Newton's text echoes the Latin hymn *Jesu dulcis memoria* (Hymn 642, page 94), attributed (probably erroneously) to the medieval mystic St. Bernard, who himself wrote a commentary on the Song of Songs.

The text is matched with a tune by a nineteenth-century English composer.

❧

When my brothers and I were little, we always looked forward to summer visits to my Grandmother Percy, who lived in rural Pennsylvania. Our days there were full of freedom. Instead of playing in a suburban back yard and a school playground, we romped in her barn and her garden, climbed in her apple trees, and roamed the meadow which bordered two sides of her property. As children usually do, we inevitably met up with minor accidents: scrapes to knees, stings inflicted by the wasps whose nests we'd disturbed, and bumps and bruises resulting from miscalculating how high we could climb or how far we could reach.

When these things would happen, Grandma Percy would hasten to her pantry and bring out a bottle filled with golden liquid. It was labeled "Oil of Gladness." I can still remember its scent; I discovered afterwards that it was probably thymol oil infused with the herb thyme, which is reputed to have healing properties. Some years later, I discovered the origin of the elixir's name. Psalm 45 was read one day in church, and when we came to verse 8—"Therefore God, your God, has anointed you with the oil of gladness above your fellows"— we could hardly contain our hilarity.

Oil of Gladness was an all-purpose remedy. It soothed bee stings and put an end to the stinging of scraped skin and soreness of bruises. But most of all, it made us feel better because of its name. It was synonymous with comfort. When we saw Grandma coming towards us with that magical bottle, we knew we would be all right.

I suppose that John Newton, living in an age of herbal medicine, probably knew something like this balm. As he looked around him, he saw people stung by disappointments, bruised by tragedies, and bloodied by life's battles. When Newton attributed to the name of Jesus the qualities of a healing ointment, he conveyed to his hearers, in a way no abstract theological language could have done, the fact that God's grace could restore them to health.

To use the name of Jesus as a healing ointment is as effective today as it was in Newton's era. When we ponder some of the divine names—Rock, Shield, Hiding-place, Shepherd, Guardian, Friend, Prophet, Priest, King, Lord, Life, Way, End—we bring his presence into our hearts. It is a presence which indeed makes our wounded spirits whole, and calms and feeds and refreshes us. Like the Oil of Gladness, it assures us that we will be all right.

Proper 18: *The Sunday closest to September 7*

Hymn 376   Joyful, joyful, we adore thee
Henry van Dyke (1852–1933)

Henry van Dyke was born in Germantown, Pennsylvania, and educated at Brooklyn Polytechnic Institute, Princeton University, and Princeton Theological Seminary. After ordination in 1879, he served the United Congregational Church in Newport, Rhode Island, for four years before moving to New York City, where he became pastor of the Brick Presbyterian Church. There, the vigor and originality of his preaching attracted large congregations. Because of his literary skills, he was appointed Murray Professor of English literature at Princeton University in 1889, remaining there until his retirement in 1923.

Van Dyke's Princeton home, "Avalon," became a gathering place of authors and intellectuals. During his tenure there, he served from 1913 to 1917 as United States minister to the Netherlands and Luxembourg at the request of President Woodrow Wilson, who had known van Dyke when Wilson was president of Princeton. In 1918, he was appointed a lieutenant commander in the United States Navy Chaplains Corps.

A prolific writer, van Dyke published approximately twenty-five books, including *The Reality of Religion* (1884), *The Poetry of Tennyson* (1889), *The Story of the Other Wise Man* (1896), and *The Gospel for an Age of Doubt* (1896). After his retirement, he devoted himself entirely to literary work. Van Dyke was the chairman of the committee that prepared the Presbyterian Church's Book of Common Worship in 1905, as well as its revision in 1932.

The author described his ideal of hymnwriting in the following lines:

> These verses are simple expressions of common Christian feelings and desires in this present time,—hymns of today that may be sung together by people who know the thought of the age, and are not afraid that any truth of science will destroy religion, or any revolution on earth overthrow the kingdom of heaven. Therefore these are hymns of trust and joy and hope.[123]

"Joyful, joyful, we adore thee" reflects the love of nature characteristic of its author. During a preaching visit to Williams College in 1907, he wrote the words of this hymn and placed them before the college president, James Garfield, at the breakfast table, with the words: "Here is a hymn for you.

Your mountains [the Berkshires] were my inspiration. It must be sung to the tune of Beethoven's "Hymn to Joy."

The text was published in *The Poems of Henry van Dyke*, in 1911, matched with the Beethoven tune, *Hymn to Joy*, as the poet intended.

☙

I have been attending an environmental ethics class taught by a professor of philosophy. As we have explored the various schools of ethics in the light of the environmental issues of today, it has become clear that our old attitudes no longer suffice. As human perspective and knowledge grow, our ethical views must include the rest of nature, for human culture is embedded in nature.

The class has come to see that we must see nature as having "intrinsic value"—another way of saying that nature has purpose in and of itself, not merely in relation to its usefulness to us. Many of the recent classes have been dedicated to exploring just what that purpose is. It is a difficult philosophical question. How can we can identify and express what gives nature intrinsic value?

In every class, I need to restrain myself, remembering that I am in a *philosophy* class, where there is a clear distinction between the philosophical enterprise and other academic disciplines. For the sake of intellectual integrity, we are expected to keep our discussion unadulterated by other realms of human endeavor. And I am also mindful that I am among people of many religious beliefs and also of none at all.

But I want to raise my hand: "Don't you see? The intrinsic value of nature lies in the fact that it too was made by the hand of God. It too is a beloved creation of God. Just as we are made to be ourselves and thus praise our Maker, so each element of nature praises its Maker in being itself!"

Human beings, from the beginning of our history, have recognized this. The first religious impulses were animistic: people venerated the sacred in nature itself. The worship of the sun, of sacred groves of trees, of the eagle or the bear, all are impulses based on the experience of otherness in the world that surrounds us, on value that is unattached to its usefulness to humanity.

I wish I could stand up and sing this hymn in philosophy class, because Henry van Dyke has expressed the Christian understanding of nature's purpose so well. Nature's purpose is to glorify God by being itself. "All thy works with joy surround thee / . . . Field and forest, vale and mountain, / blooming meadow, flashing sea, / chanting bird and flowing fountain, / call us to rejoice in thee." Not only does nature inspire us to praise the Creator; everything in nature, from the stars to the flashing sea, rejoices as well.

Van Dyke, like many poets, has revealed the human experience of being deeply embedded in the natural world through language itself. Our hearts "unfold like flowers before [the One who is] . . . ocean-depth of happy rest!" This is not the first time in Christian history that nature has provided an alternative theological vocabulary, and one that everyone can understand.

While interdisciplinary cooperation between theologians and philosophers might be useful in our classroom dilemma, that is not likely to happen in a secular institution of higher learning like ours. We can, however, make the connection for ourselves. Religion does not muddy the philosophical and ethical waters; it can, instead, give us a clear view—to the very bottom—of the truth.

When we recognize the truth of nature's intrinsic worth as a creation of God, we can forge our necessary new ethical perspective based on praise rather than duty. Through our acceptance that the human species is not alone in adoring God, we will hear our voices embedded in a vast choir made up of the rest of creation. We will be inspired to learn new ways to love and protect that creation, and thereby be lifted ever closer to the joy divine.

Proper 19: *The Sunday closest to September 14*

Hymn 689   I sought the Lord and afterward I knew
Anon., *Pilgrim Hymnal, 1904*

Raymond Glover writes, "Christian hymnody throughout the ages has been enriched by the work of poets and composers whose names are known only to God. Such is the case with this text."[124]

"I sought the Lord and afterward I knew" was first published in the late nineteenth century. The poem is subjective, with what Glover calls a "quaint but beautiful archaic charm."[125]

In the second stanza, the reference to walking yet not sinking "on the storm-vexed sea" suggests that the hymn may have been written as a meditation on the story in Matthew 14:22–33 of Peter's attempt to walk on the water toward Jesus.

Glover suggests that the theology expressed in the hymn is reminiscent of passages in the writings of Augustine of Hippo. With St. Augustine, the anonymous hymnwriter believes that it is God who "makes the first move" in attracting the soul to God—an idea expressed theologically as the doctrine of "prevenient grace."

The text is matched with a folklike tune by a contemporary American composer.

❧

In my childhood, when evening came, along with the opportunity for bedtime stories, I never tired of hearing my mother tell the story about my wandering away. I was about two years old. It was summer and I was barefoot, playing in the back yard with the neighbor's Springer Spaniel, Dutchy. Mother had thought that the gate to our fenced yard was closed and went into the house briefly, perhaps to answer a ringing telephone, or to bring out the laundry. When she came back into the yard, I was gone.

Since she did not find me in the immediate vicinity, she began to rally the neighbors, who joined in the search. As the minutes ticked by, everyone became more anxious. Finally they came across a man working in a garden beside the busy road at the end of our dead-end street. He pointed to a lane across from his house: "Yes, I saw a little girl and a dog going down Saxon Woods Road." Mother did not wait to tell him how appalled she was that he had merely watched a small barefoot child with a dog cross the dangerous street without intervening. She took off.

Saxon Woods Road at that time had few houses; it was bordered mostly by woods, a golf course, and some underbrush. And it was in that underbrush she and her friends first heard me, crying because I was lost and my bare feet had been scratched by the brambles into which I had followed Dutchy.

I do not think that, to her dying day, my mother ever got over that incident. I certainly have not forgotten it, not because I remember it myself, but because of the emotion which lay behind my mother's frequent retelling of the tale. Because it was the most dramatic occurrence of my young life up to that point, it provided a theme for annual elementary school compositions entitled: "The Day I Got Lost."

When I became a mother myself and would occasionally lose track of one of my sons in a busy store, I began to understand the emotion with which Mother related my favorite bedtime story. There is nothing as terrifying as losing one's child.

What was so comforting to me, of course, was that she found me. I was lost, and I was found.

No wonder we love the gospel parables about the shepherd who does not tire of looking for his lost sheep until he lifts it to his shoulders and comes home rejoicing. Or the woman stubbornly seeking her lost coin, and never giving up until she finds it.

When my mother gathered her tearful child up in her arms and took her home rejoicing, she also became a parable for me, the meaning of which that I have never forgotten: it is not so much that I find my Savior, but that my Savior, again and again, finds me.

Proper 20: *The Sunday closest to September 21*

Hymn 628   Help us, O Lord, to learn
William Watkins Reid, Jr. (b. 1923)

William Watkins Reid, Jr. was born in New York City and educated at Oberlin College and the Yale Divinity School. During World War II, he served in the United States Army Medical Corps, spending eight months in a German prisoner of war camp and earning three battle stars.

He was pastor for Congregational and Methodist congregations in North Dakota and Pennsylvania, and in 1978 was appointed District Superintendent for Wilkes-Barre in the United Methodist Church.

Reid is an active member of the Hymn Society in the United States and Canada. "Help us, O Lord, to learn" was written for the thirty-fifth anniversary of *The International Journal of Religious Education*. The journal collaborated with the Hymn Society in inviting hymnwriters to submit texts on Christian education. Of the almost four hundred texts received, fifteen were published in *Fifteen New Christian Education Hymns*. This text has appeared since then in a number of hymnals.

It is matched with a tune by a nineteenth-century British composer.

సొ

When I wrote my book *Praying, A Book for Children*, I tried to translate the categories of prayer I had described in *The Breath of God*, an earlier book written for adults, into language a child could understand. After I had written the chapters on "Praying with Words" (verbal prayer), "Praying by Thinking about God" (reflective prayer), and "Praying by Noticing" (contemplative prayer), I came to the category of prayer as action. How would I explain to a child what it meant to grow closer to God through the activities of daily life?

I tried to imagine the world of the children who would read my book. It was obvious that "Praying in Work and in Play" included being kind to other people, cleaning one's room, or making a get-well card for an ill neighbor, and these were akin to the adult's idea of ministry. It was also obvious that making decisions—like whether or not to join the bullies on the playground or whether to be brave enough to be the only one to throw your candy wrapper in the trash—were a part of growing in friendship with God.

But there were three other categories which I recognized were much more important parts of a child's life. One was what I called "Making and Doing Things," the equivalent of the artist's or athlete's sense of oneness with the divine that comes through exercising their special skills. "We all have gifts, and God, the Creator, loves to see us use them."[126]

The second was "Playing," just delighting in the pleasure and fun of being alive, the adult equivalent of taking time for rest and recreation. "When we take time to rest and play and enjoy life, we are, in a way, saying 'thank you' to our Creator."[127]

Third was the category in which a child of school age spends most of the hours of the day: "Learning."

> Your mind is filled with curiosity about many things. When you take the time to follow that curiosity and to learn about the world around you, you probably appreciate God's world more. So, even if going to school or doing your homework doesn't always *seem* like growing in friendship with God, it can be![128]

I regret that I had not included this final category in *The Breath of God*. I remember that when I went to seminary after many years away from school, it felt as if my brain were being reawakened, like an atrophied muscle being challenged to move after years of disuse. Ever since, I have tried to remember that learning, like aerobic exercise for the heart and lungs, keeps this "muscle" in good health.

I am convinced that learning continues to be a way to grow in love of God and in the understanding of how to relate our faith to our daily lives. This learning need not be confined to religious subjects for, as I explained to my younger readers, anything that can help us increase our understanding and appreciation of God's world will help us grow in faith.

I am probably not alone when I confess that I learn best when I have to teach someone else, through writing or in the classroom. So those of us involved in Christian education have a special privilege. We can delve into this most important field of study, "the beauty of [God's] ways," and convey what we have learned to others. In so doing, we will discover that God's laws and God's love will be inscribed both on our hearts and on the hearts of those we teach, so that both can "live a life of praise."

Proper 21: *The Sunday closest to September 28*

Hymn 346   **Completed, Lord, the Holy Mysteries**
Liturgy of St. Basil; tr. *Cyril E. Pocknee (1906–1980)*

Basil was born about 329, in Caesarea of Cappadocia, into a wealthy and distinguished Christian family. He was educated in classical Hellenism and might have continued in academic life had it not been for the faith of his sister, Macrina. He was baptized at the age of twenty-eight and ordained a deacon soon afterwards.

Inspired by Macrina, who had founded the first monastic order for women, Basil traveled to study the life of anchorites (hermit monastics) in Egypt and elsewhere, and in 358 returned to Cappadocia and founded the first monastery for men at Ibora. Assisted by Gregory Nazianzus, he compiled *The Longer and Shorter Rules*, which transformed the solitary life of the anchorites into a life in community which included both prayer and work. These guidelines became the foundation for Eastern monastic discipline.

Basil was ordained presbyter in 364 and was consecrated Bishop of Caesarea in 370. This brought him into the thick of the theological controversies of the time. Along with his brother Gregory, Bishop of Nazianzus, and his friend Gregory, Bishop of Nyssa, he championed Christian orthodoxy against the heresy known as Arianism, which denied the divinity of Christ. The three became known as the Cappadocian Fathers.

In his treatise *On the Holy Spirit*, Basil argued that both the language of Scripture and the faith of the church require that the same honor, glory, and worship is to be paid to the Spirit as to the Father and the Son.

Basil had great compassion for the poor: when he died, his will directed that a complete new town be built on his estate in Caesarea, complete with housing, a hospital, a church for the poor, and a hospice for travelers.

The Liturgy of St. Basil is very probably the work of St. Basil, since it is based on early Cappadocian practice. It is still used in the Eastern church on certain days in the ecclesiastical year in place of the ordinary "Liturgy of St. Chrysostom": on Sundays in Lent except for Palm Sunday, on Maundy Thursday, on the Eves of Easter, Christmas, and Epiphany, and on the Feast of St. Basil on January 1.

In the Liturgy, this hymn is the post-communion hymn used as the sacred vessels are cleansed. The prayer can be translated as follows:

> Completed and fulfilled as far as it is in our power,
> O Christ our God, is the mystery of your dispensation.

For we possess the memorial of your death, we saw the symbol of your Resurrection, we were filled with your unending life, we enjoyed your inexhaustible delight, of which also be pleased to make all of us worthy in the age to come. By the grace of your pre-existent Father, and your holy and good and life-giving Spirit, now and for ever and unto ages of ages, Amen.

The translation is by Cyril Pocknee, a scholarly English parish priest, who calls it "a metrical paraphrase rather than a literal translation."[129] Pocknee was chairman of the Gregorian Association and joint chairman of the Hymn Society of Great Britain and Ireland. His publications include liturgical studies, the rewriting of Percy Dearmer's *Parson's Handbook*, contributions to *A Dictionary of Liturgy and Worship*, and a compilation entitled *The French Diocesan Hymns and their Melodies*.

The text is set to a tune by Orlando Gibbons.

ꙮ

In his book *The Orthodox Church*, Kallistos Ware writes "The chief place in Christian worship belongs to the sacraments or, as they are called in the Greek, the *mysteries*. 'It is called a mystery,' writes Saint John Chrysostom of the Eucharist, 'because what we believe is not the same as what we see, but we see one thing and believe another.' This double character, at once outward and inward, is the distinctive feature of a sacrament . . . in every sacrament there is the combination of an outward visible sign with an inward spiritual grace."[130]

Although the Eastern church, like its Western sister, identifies seven major sacraments, there are many other sacramental actions, like the blessing of the waters at Epiphany and the blessing of homes. Ware continues,

Between the wider and the narrower sense of the term "sacrament" there is no rigid division: the whole Christian life must be seen as a unity, as a single mystery or one great sacrament, whose different aspects are expressed in a great variety of acts, some performed but once in a man's life, others perhaps daily.[131]

In this most mystical branch of the Christian church, the Eucharist is "other-worldly." It is celebrated using the words of liturgies from the first centuries of the Christian era, with elaborate ritual and ancient music. The liturgy does not attempt—or at least did not during the years I occasionally attended worship at a Russian Orthodox seminary—to try to be up-to-date or "relevant." It does not matter that not everybody knows all the music, or that we cannot see much of what is going on at the altar, which is hidden behind the *iconostasis*, a wall of icons. It does not matter that it is not over in an hour, or even an hour and a quarter. It does not matter *when* it is over, because the liturgy takes place in God's time, not ours.

Paradoxically, many people, including myself, find that the liturgy's "other-worldliness" is transformative. Just as God transforms bread and wine into the Body and Blood of Christ, so we who are flesh and blood can be transformed into something more than ourselves. Orthodox theologians speak of "deification" or "divinization." Although this concept may seem remote to the Western mind, its scriptural base is sound: Jesus prayed at the Last Supper, "that they may all be one. As you, Father, are in me and I am in you, may they also be in us." (Jn. 17:21). Behind this doctrine lies the idea that we are made in the image of God, and that our final goal is to share in the life of the Trinity. Everything on earth then can become sacramental: a visible sign of this invisible process.

When I remember the times I have attended Eastern Orthodox worship, I realize that the liturgy gives worshipers an opportunity to practice what "deification" feels like. Caught up in the beauty of the icons, music, incense, and movement, I have forgotten, if even for a moment, everything but God.

Proper 22: *The Sunday closest to October 5*

Hymn 541   Come, labor on
Jane Laurie Borthwick (1813–1897)

Jane Laurie Borthwick, the descendant of an old Scottish family, was the daughter of the manager of the North British Insurance Office in Edinburgh. Following a trip to the continent, her father encouraged Jane and her sister Sarah to translate German hymns. The result was *Hymns from the Land of Luther*, which included four volumes published between 1854 and 1862. They contained one hundred twenty-two hymns, sixty-one by Jane and fifty-three by Sarah. It was not long before many of these translations were printed in other hymnals, both in England and in America.

Borthwick appropriated the initials H.L.L. from the title of the book and used them as a pseudonym for many of her hymns that appeared in two subsequent volumes, *Family Treasury* and *Thoughts for Thoughtful Hours*. A collection of translations of poems by the German poet Meta Heusser-Schweizer was published in 1875 under the title of *Alpine Lyrics*.

A devoted member of the Free Church of Scotland, Borthwick was active in various religious and social causes.

"Come, labor on" was written by Borthwick for her *Thoughts for Thoughtful Hours* (1859). Using New Testament imagery, this hymn for church-workers likens the winning of souls to the harvesting of grain.

A stirring tune by T. Tertius Noble mirrors the vigor of the text.

❧

I have to admit that, at an earlier period in my life, singing this hymn exhausted me. "Come, labor on" was not the kind of thing I wanted to hear after a long week; I would have preferred a hymn about resting in Jesus' presence.

But I have learned better. I have learned that one of the great blessings of life is the opportunity to do meaningful work. When we labor at something we like to do, with the purpose of enhancing the well-being of the world, we are doing the work of God, whether or not we are the church-workers for which this hymn was written.

When I was young, I was always puzzled about the work my father did each day when he left in the morning to commute to New York City. I knew he looked like the other businessmen on the train, and, since I was much more impressed by people who were in the arts, I am sure I undervalued his work. I knew little about what he actually did as a management consultant and career counselor until after he died, when letters to my mother poured into our home. "Your husband changed my life; he directed me in the right direction toward a career which has been deeply satisfying." "His advice kept me sane." "He helped our chaotic company work again."

My father, I learned, had done God's work in a way I had

never fully realized. He had an intuitive sense of the gifts of other people and could guide them towards appropriate career paths. When it came to management consulting, he was a kind of healer, first diagnosing what was wrong in struggling organizations and then prescribing a cure. As a result, he was a much loved colleague and mentor, worthy indeed of the welcome "Servant, well done."

Frederich Beuchner writes about vocation:

> There are all different kinds of voices calling you to all different kinds of work, and the problem is to find out which is the voice of God rather than of Society, say, or the Superego, or Self-Interest.
>
> By and large a good rule for finding out is this. The kind of work God usually calls you to is the kind of work (a) that you need most to do and (b) that the world most needs to have done. . . .
>
> The place God calls you to is the place where your deep gladness and the world's deep hunger meet.[132]

The place of our deep gladness and the world's deep hunger. That is what makes labor sacred, whether it be the unsung labor of a parent caring for a child, the faithful labor of those who care for our houses and highways so that we will be secure and safe, the patient labor of the farmer or counselor, the creative labor of the artist or musician, or the skilled labor of the surgeon or physicist. All work, in their own ways, at tending the world God created, if it is a labor of love. "Servants, well done."

Proper 23: *The Sunday closest to October 12*

Hymn 415   **When all thy mercies, O my God**
Joseph Addison (1672–1719)

Joseph Addison was born in Milston, Yorkshire, the son of the dean of Lichfield. He was educated at Charterhouse and Queen's and Magdalen Colleges, Oxford, and was a fellow of Magdalen from 1698 to 1711, during which time he spent some years traveling on the continent. He was a distinguished classical scholar and his Latin poems attracted the attention of Dryden.

Although he was expected to become an Anglican clergyman, he chose instead to enter the fields of law and politics, and held several important posts, being successively a commissioner of appeals, an undersecretary of state, secretary to the Lord Lieutenant of Ireland, and chief secretary for Ireland.

He formed close friendships with Swift, Steele, and other writers and was a prominent member of the Kit-Kat Club, a gathering of leading Whigs which met in the house of a pastry cook near Temple Bar in London.

As a writer, Addison collaborated with Richard Steele in producing *The Spectator*, which appeared in 1712 and contained several of his hymns. He contributed also to *The Tatler*, *The Guardian*, and *The Freeholder*. He also wrote for the stage.

Addison said of himself, "I shall be ambitious to have it said of me, that I have brought philosophy out of closets and libraries, schools and colleges, to dwell in clubs and assemblies, at tea-tables and coffee-houses."[133] He was a great admirer of John Locke and did much to popularize his ideas.

He died at Holland House, Kensington, and is buried in Westminster Abbey.

In his sketch of Addison in *Lives of the Poets*, Samuel Johnson concluded, "Whoever wishes to attain an English style, familiar but not coarse, and elegant but not ostentatious, must give his days and nights to the volumes of Addison.[134]

This hymn appeared first in *The Spectator* in the August 9, 1712 issue, at the conclusion of an essay on "Gratitude." The heart of the essay comes in the second paragraph:

> If Gratitude is due from Man to Man, how much more from Man to his Maker! The Supreme Being does not only confer on us those Bounties which proceed more immediately from his Hand, but even those Benefits which are conveyed to us by others. Every Blessing we enjoy, by what Means soever it may be derived upon us, is the gift of him who is the great Author of Good, and Father of Mercies.[135]

The hymn's last line echoes the final line of another well-known poem written one hundred years earlier by George Herbert, whose "King of glory, King of peace, ends with "e'en eternity's too short to extol thee" (Hymn 382, *The Hymnal 1982*). Addison's text has long been popular. For the past two centuries, nearly every significant hymn collection has included some part of it.

The text is matched with a seventeenth-century psalm tune.

☙

Addison's hymn helps me understand that, just as we can cultivate practical habits that enhance our health, like eating a well-balanced diet or getting enough sleep, we can also cultivate habits of thought. These habits may well have an impact upon our overall health that is just as great as those practices encouraged by our doctors.

Mental habits affect the way we see our lives. It is as if we had a choice of prescriptions for corrective lenses, each one causing us to view the world in a different way.

It does not take long to guess the lenses through which people are viewing the world. Watch what they look for first, and how their energy increases as they speak about it. Most of these habits are of such long-standing that people are not conscious of them.

Perhaps it is the "victim" prescription. In every encounter, the victim is on the lookout for being ill-treated. If you speak with a victim, you will hear new energy when the subject matter is an occasion of feeling unjustly used.

Or perhaps it is the "discontent" prescription. Nothing is quite right. Everything could be better: the house could be a different size, colleagues at work more cooperative, the body a different size or age.

Addison reveals his mental prescription immediately in this hymn. His is the habit of gratitude. When he looks out at the world, he is transported with the view. This is his regular habit. "Ten thousand thousand precious gifts / my daily thanks employ." He is lost in "wonder, love, and praise."

Addison's habit has a physical effect. His gratitude is somatic. Warmth "glows" within his fervent heart; he "tastes" God's gifts with joy. His gratitude provides so much energy that it overflows: "but oh, eternity's too short / to utter all thy praise!"

I have always been intrigued by the story of Jesus healing the ten lepers. Only one of them had the habit of gratitude; only one returned to give him thanks. It was to this one leper that Jesus said, "Your faith has made you well." The others were healed of leprosy; the one with the habit of gratitude was more than that. He was *well*.

The good news is that it is never too late to cultivate this habit. First we need to recognize what our old "prescription" is, and decide whether it is a healthy one through which to view the world. Should we discover that it is not, we need to adjust to new lenses by using them regularly and intentionally. Eventually our vision will change, and we will recognize, in our ever-grateful hearts, that we have been made well.

Proper 24: *The Sunday closest to October 19*

Hymn 638,639   Come, O thou Traveler unknown
Charles Wesley (1707–1788)*

"Come, O thou Traveler unknown," entitled by Charles Wesley "Wrestling Jacob," was first published in John and Charles Wesley's *Hymns and Sacred Poems* in 1742. The poem is based on the story in Genesis 32:24–30:

> Jacob was left alone; and a man wrestled with him until daybreak. When the man saw that he did not prevail against Jacob, he struck him on the hip socket; and Jacob's hip was put out of joint as he wrestled with him. Then he said, "Let me go, for the day is breaking." But Jacob said, "I will not let you go, unless you bless me." So he said to him, "What is your name?" And he said, "Jacob." Then the man said, "You shall no longer be called Jacob, but Israel, for you have

------

*For additional biographical information, see *A Closer Walk*, 182–184.

striven with God and with humans, and have prevailed. Then Jacob asked him, "Please tell me your name." But he said, "Why is it that you ask my name?" And there he blessed him. So Jacob called the place Peniel, saying "For I have seen God face to face, and yet my life is preserved."

Charles Wesley's *Journal* records that he preached on this Scripture passage eight times between May 1741 and January 1749. He has interpreted the story christologically, which is especially clear in the stanzas which have been omitted. In the original stanza three, Jacob asks the stranger, "Art Thou the Man that died for me?" In stanza eleven, he proclaims, "I know Thee, Saviour, who Thou art, / Jesus, the feeble Sinner's friend."[136]

In John Wesley's obituary tribute to his brother at the Methodist Conference of 1788, he acknowledged, "Dr. Watts did not scruple to say that that single poem, 'Wrestling Jacob,' was worth all the verses he himself had written."[137]

The text is matched with an American folk melody and also with a tune written especially for the text by the twentieth-century Erik Routley.

❧

Anyone who has taken religion seriously has, like Jacob, wrestled with God.

The wrestling may be caused by occurrences or passages in our lives. Perhaps a tragedy has occurred, and we rail at a God who is supposed to be the Good Shepherd, keeping us and those we love from harm. Or we have lost our job and we struggle with our sense of identity and vocation. Or, weighed down by too many burdens, we feel deep animosity against life itself, which seems pointless and depressing.

But the wrestling may have little obvious outward cause. It may be caused instead by inner spiritual changes. In the natural process of growth, our images of God inevitably change. We felt comfortable with our old conceptions of God, and we are loathe to let them go. All the trappings of religion which may have been our mainstay may lose their meaning; our "company before is gone." Now we are alone, and it feels like being in a desert. God is, suddenly, not a familiar figure, but a "Traveler unknown." We tussle with this mysterious stranger and insist, "Who are you?"

The sixteenth-century Spanish mystic John of the Cross speaks of the "Dark night of the soul": "Souls begin to enter the dark night when God is drawing them out of the state of beginners."[138]

> During the aridities of the night of sense—when God effects the change of which I have spoken . . . spiritual persons have to endure great afflictions, not so much because of aridity, but because they are afraid that they will be lost on this road; thinking that they are spiritually ruined, and that God has forsaken them, because they find no help or consolation in holy things.[139]

John of the Cross reminds us how painful it can be to no longer find pleasure in our religious practices and to outgrow our images of God. These are times of great struggle.

However, this struggle is like isometric exercise, when we move in such a way that our muscles are strengthened through resistance. If we are training physically, we might try to do this through push-ups, building up our biceps by pushing against the floor. Or we can take up wrestling, pushing against our opponent!

Our times of wrestling with God are not times when our faith is waning; rather, they are like the isometric exercise of the soul. When we resist easy answers, we are building up our faith, just as the gymnast builds up muscle tone. However, unlike the world of sports, this match is not with an opponent but with an ally, and winning is not the goal.

It is God's own self who engages us, helping us to grow, whether we are aware of it or not. And the goal is to live and pray, more and more, strengthened by the unknown Traveler whose name is Universal Love.

Proper 25: The Sunday closest to October 26

Hymn 561   Stand up, stand up, for Jesus
George Duffield, Jr. (1818–1888)

George Duffield was born in Carlisle, Pennsylvania, and educated at Yale University and the Union Theological Seminary. He was pastor of Presbyterian churches in Brooklyn, New York, Bloomfield, New Jersey, and Philadelphia, Pennsylvania, before he moved to the Midwest, where he served churches in Illinois and Michigan. For seven years, he was a regent of the University of Michigan. Independently wealthy, he devoted much of his life to evangelism and to establishing small congregations. He was editor of a Presbyterian family newspaper, the *Christian Observer*.

Duffield summarized the origin of this hymn in a letter dated May 29, 1883:

"Stand up for Jesus" was the dying message of the Rev. Dudley A. Tyng to the Young Men's Christian Association, and the ministers associated with them during the great revival of 1853, in the Noon-Day Prayer Meeting, usually known as "The Work of God in Philadelphia."

A very dear personal friend, I know young Tyng as one of the noblest, bravest, manliest men I ever met. . . . The Sabbath before his death he preached in the immense edifice known as Jaynes' Hall, one of the most successful sermons of modern times. Of the five thousand men there assembled, at least one thousand, it was believed, were "the slain of the Lord." His text was Exodus 10:11, and hence the allusion in the third verse of the hymn.

The following Wednesday, leaving his study for a moment, he went to the barn floor, where a mule was at work on a horse-power, shelling corn. Patting him on the neck, the sleeve of his silk study gown caught in the cogs of the wheel, and his arm was torn out by the roots! His death occurred in a few hours. . . .

The following Sunday the author of the hymn preached from Eph. 6:14, and the above verses were written simply as the concluding exhortation. The superintendent of the Sabbath school had a fly-leaf printed for the children—a stray copy found its way into a Baptist newspaper—and from that paper it has gone in English, and in German and Latin translations all over the world.[140]

It has been conjectured that since Tyng had been perse-cuted for his stand against slavery, he implied in his hymn that the singers should "Stand up for Jesus in the person of the down-trodden slave."[141] The militant mood concerning the issue of slavery is probably responsible for the extensive militaristic imagery that permeates this text.

First published as a broadside, the hymn became popular immediately and soon found its way into Baptist, Presbyterian, and Episcopal hymnals.

It is matched with an energetic tune with which it has been associated since 1861.

❧

How I loved this hymn when I was in Sunday school! Like "Awake, my soul", it helped me stretch every muscle. Even its military imagery appealed to me, because these were the days of World War II, when patriotism was high and war seemed the obvious alternative to a world dominated by the Nazis. It was quite clear to us that God was on our side.

Things are different now. With the advent of nuclear weapons, the stakes have become higher. Military conflict in our day is painted in shades of grey rather than in black and white, and most thinking people choose to see the role of the armed forces as a peacekeeping one.

So what do I make of "Stand up, stand up, for Jesus"?

For one thing, the image of battle has become more relevant the more I have been involved in local political issues. Our town lies in the midst of fertile farmland, which is threatened by so-called "development," much opposed by the people who live in this region, with the exception of some developers who stand to gain financially and public officials who stand to gain politically. This quiet part of northern Ohio is a battleground, although it doesn't appear that way to the naked eye. Will the decisions made about the land honor the will of the citizens who live here, or will they impose the will of those who want to gain more political or financial power?

When I became involved in these issues, it did indeed feel like standing up for Jesus, the Word who was "in the beginning" at the creation of this beautiful world. Noting that the powerless were the ones who would lose if the developers had their way, and that God's gifts are intended to be shared with equity and justice, I found that I had to "stand up," however loath I am temperamentally to enter into conflict.

During this period, I have been reminded that "standing" is an excellent metaphor for bearing witness. For one thing, the "military posture"—shoulders back, chest expanded, spine ramrod straight—is not conducive to standing for very long. Instead, I have learned that proper stance is a matter of centering the body weight over the feet, of aligning the pelvis and shoulder girdle over the center of gravity, and of holding my head erect but relaxed, as if a string attached to my skull were being pulled upward. That way, I am in touch with my foundation: my weight upon the earth. And that way, I can breathe, because my shoulders are pulled down gently by the shoulder blades and the ribs can move freely, allowing the lungs to expand. Nor do I try to eradicate the natural curves of the spine, which are there to absorb the physical shocks of walking or jumping.

Like those who study the physical act of standing, those who are involved in the battle with evil need to align ourselves with our foundation in God, as solid as the body weight pulled towards the floor by the force of gravity. We need to stand so that we do not block—by our very effort to stand tall—our breathing of the renewing spirit of God. Our hearts and spirits need to remain flexible, rather than ramrod straight, so that we can be resilient, absorbing the impacts of conflict without harm.

A tall order! But we do not accomplish this alone. "Stand up, stand up, for Jesus; / stand in his strength alone; / the arm of flesh will fail you, / ye dare not trust your own; / put on the Gospel armor, / and watching unto prayer, / when duty calls, or danger, / be never wanting there."

All Saints' Day: November 1

Hymn 286   Who are these like stars appearing?
Theobald Heinrich Schenck (1656–1727); tr. *Frances Elizabeth Cox (1812–1897)*

Theobald Heinrich Schenck was born in Heidelbach, Hesse, Germany, the son of a pastor in the town. He was educated at the Pädagogium at Giessen and at the University of Giessen. He returned to the Pädagogium as a master from 1676 to 1679, when he was ordained as town preacher and *definitor* at the Stadtkirche in Giessen. "Who are these like stars appearing?" is his only known hymn text. The twenty-stanza poem first appeared in *Neuvermehrtes Gesangbüchlein*, published in Frankfurt-am-Main in 1719.

The translator, Frances Elizabeth Cox, was an Englishwoman born in Oxford and noted for her translations of German hymns. With the encouragement of the German ambassador to England, Baron Bunsen, she published in 1841 *Sacred Hymns from the German*, which contains her translation of fourteen stanzas of "Who are these like stars appearing." In 1864, a subsequent volume, *Hymns from the*

German, was printed. Cox herself chose the present five stanzas for the hymn's publication in Henry Alford's *Psalms and Hymns*, and they have been included in every *Hymnal* since 1892.

The text is based on Revelation 7:13–17:

> Then one of the elders addressed me, saying, "Who are these, robed in white, and where have they come from?" I said to him, "Sir, you are the one that knows." Then he said to me, "These are they who have come out of the great ordeal; they have washed their robes and made them white in the blood of the Lamb.
>
> For this reason they are before the throne of God,
> and worship him day and night within his temple,
> and the one who is seated on the throne will shelter them.
>
> They will hunger no more, and thirst no more,
> the sun will not strike them,
> nor any scorching heat;
>
> for the Lamb at the center of the throne will be their shepherd,
> and he will guide them to the springs of the water of life,
> and God will wipe away every tear from their eyes."

The hymn text has been matched with its seventeenth-century chorale since 1892.

⁂

Theobald Heinrich Schenck compares the saints in heaven to the stars that adorn the night sky. Like the constellations on a clear night, the saints dazzle us.

It is interesting that we have appropriated the word "star" for celebrities who dazzle us today. The adolescent practicing basketball in order to emulate his favorite player, the young woman imitating the hairstyle of her preferred television actress, the people who pore through glossy magazines, all find enjoyment in seeking the presence, through imitation or adulation, of people who are bigger than life.

The unfortunate thing is that these stars come and go, as anyone knows who has watched *Sunset Boulevard*, a movie about a fading actress desperately trying to hold on to her place in the cinematic constellation.

The stars who are part of the constellation called the Communion of Saints are never extinguished. They are the faithful who have passed before us into the presence of God. You can find their names in the Bible or in the church calendar, and often churches are named after them. But there are others who are unsung and unknown, who have also been true to their God throughout their earthly pilgrimage. They, also, have wrestled with life, have striven in prayer, and have watched and waited, dedicating their days to a good beyond their own needs and desires.

Some of them still live among us. We sometimes consider death a necessary requirement for sainthood, but it is likely that, when we consider the people who are our personal "stars," as opposed to the media "stars," we will discover otherwise.

I, for one, have an ever-increasing list of saints. They are not all found in the church calendar, not even in *Lesser Feasts and Fasts*. They are the people who have shone in my life, inspiring me to grow into the person God calls me to be.

I discovered that I had such a list when I filled out my application to seminary, in which we were asked to identify the people who had been influential in our lives.

It was an illuminating task. I discovered memories of parental love, which could not have failed to be an prelude for my later understanding of the love of God. In my imagination, I became a kindergartner again, joining a Sunday school choir led by a lady with a kind face and a red hat, who taught us about Jesus as we practiced our songs. My musings took me face to face with former teachers who nurtured my abilities in music or dance or writing and gave me the tools and the self-confidence to develop talents that may otherwise have lain dormant.

My list grew, as I remembered friends and colleagues because of the examples they set of self-giving, faithfulness, and prophetic vision. And I realized that my husband and children became my "saints" as well, both accepting me as I am and helping me to grow.

While I feel close to many of the saints celebrated liturgically during the church year, these flesh and blood saints are my particular "stars." Some of them, indeed, are now living "in God's most holy place." Whether they are now in life or in death, I know with gratitude that my relationship with them has taught me about my path and guided my steps, and that their light still illuminates my life and my prayer.

Proper 26: *The Sunday closest to November 2*

Hymn 634   I call on thee, Lord Jesus
Miles Coverdale (1487–1568)

Miles Coverdale was born in York. Ordained a priest in 1514, he entered the house of the Augustinian friars in Cambridge, where he became an enthusiast for ecclesiastical reform. After preaching against confession and images, he was forced go into exile.

In 1535, he produced on the Continent the first complete Bible to be printed in English. It drew from several sources, among them the Latin Vulgate, Martin Luther's German Bible, and Tyndale's translations of the Pentateuch and the New Testament. His translation of the psalms was for many years used in the Book of Common Prayer; it has been commented that "even in their obscure moments they have the mellow beauty of some ancient, familiar window with slightly jumbled glass; one would scarcely have the imperfections set right."[142]

The next year, still on the Continent, he produced a volume containing mainly translations of German Lutheran hymns with their melodies, entitled *Goostly psalmes and spirituall songes drawen out of the holy Scripture, for the comforte and consolacyon of soch as love to reioyse in God and his worde.*

When he returned to England, he preached throughout the West Country in order to pacify the rebellions there; in 1551, Edward VI rewarded him with the bishopric of Exeter. During the reign of Queen Mary, he again went into exile, first to Denmark, then to Germany, and finally to Geneva, where he collaborated in producing the Genevan Bible of 1560. In 1559, he returned to England in time to help in the consecration of Elizabeth I's archbishop, Matthew Parker. He chose not to return to Exeter, instead becoming rector of the parish of St. Magnus in London, "revered as a patriarch by all Protestants."[143] Two years before his death, he also resigned even this benefice, thinking it incompatible with his leadership of the nascent Puritan school of thought.

"I call on thee, Lord Jesus Christ," the earliest English hymn in *The Hymnal 1982*, appears in Coverdale's *Goostly psalmes and spirituall songes*. It is a translation of stanza one of a hymn, *Ich ruf zu dir, Herr Jesu Christ*, written by Johann Agricola, a German reformer and disciple of Martin Luther.

The text is matched with the German chorale tune with which it has historically been associated.

☙

This hymn text of utter dependence upon the Lord Jesus Christ is deceptively simple. As with so many "simple" things, like contemplative prayer or unconditional love, it is also one of the most difficult things imaginable.

If, as the theologian Schleiermacher writes, religion is "the feeling of absolute dependence,"[144] Miles Coverdale and Johann Agricola have helped us enter into faith's very heart.

Most of us do not like to admit that we are utterly dependent. This is a quality about which children can teach us a great deal, and perhaps is what Jesus meant when he said, "Whoever does not receive the kingdom of God like a child shall not enter it." (Mk. 10:15) Children have no choice but to acknowledge their dependence; human offspring are helpless for much longer than the young of other mammals. Coverdale's text would be far easier for a three-year-old, who needs her parents' help in order to survive and their attentive care in order to blossom, than it is for us.

As adults, it is only the spiritually mature who acknowledge the reality of our dependence, not only upon one another, but, above all, upon God. It is a giant step on the spiritual path to be able to say, "I have none other help but thee. / My heart is never set at rest / till thy sweet word have comforted me," something it would be very simple for a three-year-old to say to his mother, although perhaps not in Coverdale's sixteenth-century English!

Carlo Carretto, a member of the order of the Little Brothers of Charles de Foucauld, writes that he learned in the desert "an extraordinary prayer of Charles de Foucauld, a prayer summing up my whole faith, a prayer so drastic in content that I could only recite it under the impulsion of the Holy Spirit. . . . Try reciting it yourself, and see if you succeed in getting right to the end in love and peace of spirit."[145]

Here it is:

> Father,
>
> I abandon myself into your hands;
> do with me what you will.
> Whatever you may do, I thank you:
> I am ready for all, I accept all.
>
> Let only your will be done in me,
> and in all your creatures.
> I wish no more than this, O Lord.
>
> Into your hands I commend my soul;
> I offer it to you
> with all the love of my heart,
> for I love you, Lord,
> and so need to give myself,

> to surrender myself into your hands,
> without reserve,
> and with boundless confidence,
> for you are my Father.[146]

We adults would do well to take Carretto's advice, by reciting, ourselves, de Foucauld's prayer as well as Coverdale's poem, both so simple yet so drastic in content.

Proper 27: The Sunday closest to November 9

Hymn 526   Let saints on earth in concert sing
Charles Wesley (1707–1788)*

"Let saints on earth in concert sing" is part of the first hymn in Charles Wesley's anonymously published *Funeral Hymns: Second Series*, published in London in 1759. It has been much altered from the original, which includes the following:

> Ten thousand to their endless home
>   This solemn moment fly;
> And we are to the margin come,
>   And we expect to die;
> His militant embodied host,
>   With wishful looks we stand,
> And long to see that happy coast,
>   And reach the heavenly land.
>
> Our old companions in distress
>   We haste again to see,

---

*For additional biographical background, see *A Closer Walk*, 182–184.

And eager long for our release,
　　And full felicity:
Even now by faith we join our hands
　　With those that went before;
And greet the blood-besprinkled bands
　　On the eternal shore.

Our spirits too shall quickly join,
　　Like theirs, with glory crowned,
And shout to hear our Captain's sign,
　　To hear His trumpet sound:
O that we now might grasp our Guide!
　　O that the word were given!
Come, Lord of Hosts, the waves divide,
　　And land us all in heaven.[147]

The text is matched with a seventeenth-century Scottish psalter tune.

∽

In the Apostles' Creed, said at the daily offices of Morning Prayer and Evening Prayer, worshipers recite, "I believe in the communion of saints."[148] What does this mean?

In *Markings*, the spiritual journal of the late Secretary General of the United Nations, Dag Hammarskjöld, the statesman writes:

> Yet, through me there flashes this vision of a magnetic field in the soul, created in a timeless present by unknown multitudes, living in holy obedience, whose words and actions are a timeless prayer.—"The Communion of Saints"—and—within it—an eternal life.[149]

Hammarskjöld's intuition is part of a long tradition of the belief, not confined to Christianity, that those who have lived before us in time are connected in some way to us. We are together with them, just as we are together with those who may live far away but share our planet.

This idea takes various forms, depending on the culture in which it is found. In Ninian Smart's book about world religions, *The Long Search*, he writes of Africa that

> . . . the land echoes with the voices of ancestors. . . . They are part of man's ongoing life, for they are part of society—a society, though, which transcends the visibly present group. . . . But the ancestors are more than invisible members of the ongoing social order. They are the living-dead and as such they are interpreters, intermediaries, ambassadors even. For they are closer than we to the spirit world and can the more easily commune with divinities and with God."[150]

The foregoing paragraph could have served, with very few modifications, to describe the widespread devotion to departed saints during the Middle Ages, when pilgrims undertook long journeys to worship at the shrines of their favorite saints and ask for their prayers.

Charles Wesley's hymn, however, applies, not to the canonized saints of the church, but to the "unknown multitudes . . . whose words and actions are a timeless prayer" of Dag Hammarskjöld's journal.

Wesley pictures the living and the dead as divided merely by a narrow stream, across which we can easily join our hands. We are also close enough to them that we join their song and they join ours.

Hammarskjöld experienced the presence of the communion of saints as a "magnetic field" in the soul. Within his solitary and very private interior life, he felt bound to these holy companions through their prayer. The narrow stream of death was no obstacle, since the connection occurred in the unseen, eternal part of the statesman's own being.

Both writers were in the lineage of the early Christians, who painted figures called *Orants* (from the Latin word *ora*, to pray) in their hiding places in the catacombs. They are portraits of the dead, represented as if alive, with hands upraised in the act of prayer. For Christians living under persecution, these images of departed friends and family members continuing to pray for them were a great source of strength.

It is not uncommon for the dying to focus their gaze on something—or someone—unseen by onlookers, or even to greet those who have gone before. These experiences remind us of the power and comfort of the belief that we, the living and the dead, are one extended family, bound together in the eternal presence of God.

Proper 28: The Sunday closest to November 16

Hymn 600,601   O day of God, draw nigh
Robert Balgarnie Young Scott (1899–1987)

Robert B. Y. Scott was born in Toronto, Canada, and educated at the University of Toronto and at Union College, Toronto. He was ordained in the United Church of Canada in 1926 and served a church in Ontario until he left to become professor of Old Testament at Union College. He remained there until 1931. He held a similar post at United College, McGill University, Montreal for the next twenty-four years. In 1955, he was named Danforth Professor of

Religion at Princeton University, where he taught until he retired in 1968.

Scott received four honorary doctorates and many professional awards, including the Canadian Council of Churches Prize for the Centennial Hymn (1967).

His many scholarly publications include *The Original Language of the Apocalypse* (1928) and *Treasures from Judean Caves* (1955). He was the author of Vol. 5 of *The Interpreter's Bible*, which covers Isaiah 1–39.

He was in the armed forces in World War I and served as a chaplain in World War II; afterwards, he became an indefatigable writer and speaker in the cause of peace. Throughout the span of his life, he composed ten hymns, which are published in over thirty hymnals.

His best known hymns are dedicated to the cause of social justice and peace, with an emphasis on Christian responsibility to the human community. "O day of God, draw nigh" is an example. It was composed for the Fellowship for a Christian Social Order in 1937, and was included in *The Hymnal 1940* because of its message of hope for peace on the verge of the cataclysm that would become World War II.

A commentator for the 1940 hymnal criticized the hymn on the grounds that "[Scott's] concept of the 'Day of God' is in marked contrast to that of the Old Testament prophets as expressed in Zephaniah 1:14–18."[151] ("That day will be a day of wrath, a day of distress and anguish, a day of ruin and devastation, a day of darkness and gloom, a day of clouds and thick darkness. . . . " Zeph. 1:15) Such a charge seems ludicrous today, especially in view of Scott's international status as an Old Testament scholar.

Two tunes are provided: the Canadian tune that was first used with the text in *The Hymnal 1940*, and a Geneva Psalter tune, although one commentator suggests using the text with the Southern shape-note tune LANDAFF, as found in *Hymnal Supplement II*.[152]

&

"Wait 'till your father comes home!"

At the times when I am most disillusioned with humanity, I sometimes think that a reenactment of the legend of Noah's flood might be a good idea. It can be therapeutic to imagine all the stupidity and evil of which our species is capable wiped off the face of the earth through a great flood or a similarly effective catastrophe.

During those cantankerous moods, I can find soul-brothers in certain of the Hebrew prophets. Zephaniah was only one of many who threatened that humanity's wrongdoings would result in a day of doom. Malachi predicted, "See, the day is coming, burning like an oven, when all the arrogant and all evildoers will be stubble." (Mal.4:1) We can compare their frustration with the fatigued and defeated mother who —in the days when gender stereotypes were still firmly in place—would finally announce to her misbehaving offspring the dreaded, "Wait 'till your father comes home!"

Even Jesus, as we hear him through the evangelist Luke, spoke of the time when "Nation will rise against nation, and kingdom against kingdom; there will be great earthquakes, and in various places famines and pestilences; and there will be terrors and great signs from heaven." (Lk. 21:10–11)

"Wait 'till your father comes home!" Despite the era in which I was brought up, my mother never said that. Instead, as evening drew near, my brothers and I would keep our ears open for the turn of the front doorknob and then compete with one another to be the first to fling ourselves into his arms. "Daddy's home!"

So perhaps it is no surprise that, despite my envisioning the wiping out of what may be mistakenly called "civilization" on my darkest days, I find Robert B.Y. Scott's benign understanding of the day of the God to be much more congenial.

For one thing, Scott's "day of God" is not a cataclysmic event that ends history. Instead, like the stable presence of my father each evening, it is an infusion of the divine power into "our present hour."

Nor is it a time of punishment, but a time of transformation. Scott is a natural psychologist, who knew that human wrongdoing usually was the result of some kind of fear, and that the first step in mending the world was to bring the quiet of a steadfast faith to troubled minds.

God's stabilizing presence would enable humanity to build a different kind of world than the one we know: one in which justice and peace reign.

Scott, who knew the horrors of both world wars, would have had good reason to say, with the prophets, "Wait 'till your father comes home." The fact that he holds before us the possibility of change gives me hope: God has not given up on us, so we should not give up on ourselves, either. Even when we are most despairing of humanity, we can hold on to that hope, and live and work for the kingdom of peace and justice which Jesus proclaimed.

Proper 29: The Sunday closest to November 23

Hymn 478   **Jesus, our mighty Lord**
Clement of Alexandria (170?–220?); para. F. Bland Tucker
(1895–1984)***

This, one of the earliest of known Christian hymns, is the work of Clement of Alexandria, who attached it to a prose volume called *Paedagogus* (variously translated as "The Pedagogue," "The Instructor," or "The Tutor"). The goal of the book was the instruction of new converts about how to regulate their conduct in accord with their new-found faith. It was a difficult task. Clement believed that it required self-conquest, direction, integration, and obedience to Christ's new law of love.

Clement spares no detail, as is revealed in the following list of subjects he treats:

> Against embellishing the body; with whom we are to associate; behaviour in the public baths; exercises suited to a good life; clothes [simple, white]; ear-rings [no], finger-rings [yes]; hair [not long, a beard]; painting the face [no]; walking [grave and leisurely]; amusements [don't loaf in barber shops, or throw dice]; public spectacles [no]; going to church; conduct out of church; the government of the eyes; love and the kiss of charity.[153]

At the end, Clement appends a poem of thanksgiving and praise to the Instructor (the Logos. A literal translation follows:

---

*For additional biographical information, see *A Closer Walk*, 98–99.
**For additional biographical information, see *A Closer Walk*, 40–41.

Bridle of colts untamed,
Wing of unwandering birds,
Sure helm of ships,
Shepherd of royal lambs,
Assemble thy simple children to praise
holily, to hymn guilelessly with innocent
mouths, Christ the guide of children.

O King of Saints, all-subduing Word of the most high
Father, Ruler of Wisdom, support of sorrows, rejoicing in eternity, Jesus, Saviour of the human race, Shepherd, Husbandman, Helm, Bridle, Heavenly Wing of
the all-holy flock, Fisher of men who are saved, catch-
ing the chaste fishes with sweet life from the hateful
wave of the sea of vices—Guide us, Shepherd of rational sheep; guide, O Holy King, thy children safely
along the footsteps of Christ; O heavenly Way, perennial Word, immeasurable Age, eternal Light, Fount of
mercy, Performer of virtue.

Noble is the life of those who hymn God, O Christ
Jesus, heavenly milk of the sweet breasts of the graces
of the Bride, pressed out of thy wisdom. Babes nour-
ished with tender mouths, filled with the dewy spirit of
the rational pap, let us sing together simple praises,
true hymns to Christ our King, holy fee for the teaching of life; let us sing in simplicity the powerful Child.

O choir of peace, the Christ-begotten,
O chaste people, let us sing together the God of peace.[154]

Clement did not write for the "tender youth" reared in a
Christian family, but for the converts who were trying to re-
pattern their lives in what he considered the immoral environ-

ment of Alexandria. Throughout the hymn, Clement gives the Logos twenty-one different titles, each expressing some function necessary for the training of Christians.

Clement's hymn, paraphrased by F. Bland Tucker, appeared as "Master of eager youth" in previous hymnals. *The Hymnal 1982* has omitted the first of his four stanzas.

The music is a tune adapted by Ralph Vaughan Williams from an English folk melody.

ℰℐ

I wonder if the members of the Text Committee for *The Hymnal 1982* who decided to omit the first stanza of Clement of Alexandria's hymn had ever raised children. Clement would have understood the rainy days when our two young sons roared through the living room like colts untamed. He would have understood our prayers that they be protected by another Shepherd during the years when they were seeking their own paths in the world, rightly refusing our attempts to treat them like royal lambs.

It may not be theologically fashionable these days to envision Christ, the Logos, as the one who guides, subdues, bridles, and provides a helm for our children. But if we do not help our children give that task to Christ, it will be eagerly usurped by others.

There are subtle and not-so-subtle forces in society, mightily skilled in manipulating our sons and daughters by holding up role models for them to emulate. As merchandising has become more and more a shaper of culture, you can discover these role models by walking down the aisles of a toy store. Rows of impossibly svelte Barbie dolls challenge the body image of all but the anorexic female child. The heros of the hour, from Davy Crocket in my own childhood to Pokémon today, capture the imaginations of the little boys. On school playgrounds, the superheroes come to life in the play of the "colts untamed" who find in them a channel for their energy and sense of fantasy.

The world of the adolescent is even more controlled by consumer culture, whether the merchandise comes in the form of fashion or rock music. Peer pressure often subdues personal preference, and youth often find themselves floundering, without values, goals, or self-esteem.

We all need an image of the person we wish to grow into. In the long run, of course, that person is the person God created us to be. As we are seeking that true self, what better guide than the Logos, the guide of children?

In all of us, young and old, there are things that need to be subdued: selfishness, violence, envy, thoughtlessness, to name a few. It is likely that all of us have a portion of untamed colt within us. We all need to direct our raw energy so that it enhances our lives and the lives of others, rather than letting others in the society decide how we are to act and who we are to become. That is true of us, whether we are toddlers or senior adults.

What better guide can we choose than the One who said "I am the Way, the Truth, and the Life," and who keeps his children in love to life unending?

Thanksgiving Day

Hymn 705   As those of old their first fruits brought
Frank von Christierson (1900–1996)*

This text by Frank von Christierson, a Presbyterian pastor and poet, first appeared in *Ten New Stewardship Hymns*, published in New York in 1961 by the Hymn Society of America. The volume was produced in cooperation with the Department of Stewardship and Benevolence of the National Council of Churches of Christ in the U.S.A. for the observance of the fortieth anniversary of the department. It is included in an anthology of the author's texts, *Make a Joyful Noise*, published in 1987.

About the text, Christierson wrote:

> As pastor of two small churches, with small memberships and great financial needs, I have been deeply concerned with stewardship, also because I am deeply concerned about missions and the outreach of the church to "all the world," also because stewardship is a very important phase of the Christian life. No one is deeply Christian until he is a "good steward."[155]

The text is paired with an English folk melody arranged by Ralph Vaughan Williams.

ख

In contemporary urban society, agriculture is taken for granted. The first fruits of vineyard, flock, and field are found in the

---

*For additional biographical information, see *Awake, My Soul!*, 214–215.

wine, meat, and vegetable sections of the supermarket, often neatly packaged in Styrofoam and plastic wrap. Our labor consists mainly in dropping the packages into our shopping carts, waiting in line at the checkout, and paying for them.

This hymn text reminds us of something that farmers and other residents of rural areas already know about: the hard labor that produced these first fruits, with all the delight that harvest time brings. My husband and I have learned this, as parents learn so many things, from one of our children. Our older son has been deeply involved in the growing of food since he graduated from college. He studied organic gardening in a well-known program in Santa Cruz, California, and has gardened and taught gardening in various intentional communities across the United States. Organic gardening, since it eschews chemical herbicides and (often) mechanized tilling and harvesting, is extremely labor-intensive. When we visit him, we are usually enlisted to plant, weed, or harvest. For us, it is a vacation from our usual lives, since we tend only a small vegetable garden and depend on a local community farm for most of our fresh summer produce.

But for our son and his garden colleagues, it is a year-long labor of love. They never take the harvest for granted, because months of bending over the soil has preceded every head of lettuce, every eggplant, and every ear of corn.

"Those of old" used organic gardening techniques, of course, rather than modern factory farming methods. So bringing their first-fruits—actually a tenth, or tithe, of what their fields produced—to God was a substantial offering. It was no light matter.

Like these ancestors, we are called to give our first fruits to God: not merely by sharing our food, but also the wealth in our homes and in our marketplaces. We no longer do this by taking our gifts to the temple as a sacrifice. Instead, we share them with those in the world who are in destitution: a figure that is, shockingly, approximately one-fifth of the world's population. "A world in need now summons us / to labor, love, and give."

It is not only our possessions that we are summoned to share. It is, above all, our lives that are our offerings to God "that all may live." Our time and energy, our talents and our choice of occupation, are the first fruits that God wants.

None of these offerings are actually ours, of course, but God's gifts, given back to God through sharing them with others. In this labor, we imitate Christ, who gave himself so abundantly.

This offering, like organic farming, is no light matter. It takes work: heart-work and soul-work. To share our lives in this way runs counter to the grain of our self-indulgent culture. We can do it only with God's grace, through our prayer, "O thou who gavest us thyself / in Jesus Christ thy Son, / help us to give ourselves each day / until life's work is done."

Index of *Authors, Translators, and Sources*

A Closer Walk   **A**
Awake, My Soul!   **B**
New Every Morning   **C**

(Hymn numbers are in Roman type, page numbers in *italic*.)

Index of First Lines

Notes

1. Albert C. Ronander and Ethel K. Porter, *Guide to the Pilgrim Hymnal* (Philadelphia and Boston: United Church Press, 1966), 106.

2. Ronander and Porter, 98.

3. Ibid.

4. Ibid., 99.

5. Ulrich Siegfried Leupold, ed. *Liturgy and Hymns.* Vol. LIII of *Luther's Works.* (Philadelphia: Fortress Press, 1965). Quoted in Marilyn Kay Stulken, *Hymnal Companion to the Lutheran Book of Worship* (Philadelphia: Fortress Press, 1981), 153.

6. Marilyn Kay Stulken, *Hymnal Companion to the Lutheran Book of Worship* (Philadelphia: Fortress Press, 1981), 153.

7. Raymond F. Glover, ed. *The Hymnal 1982 Companion, Vol. Three A* (New York: The Church Hymnal Corporation, 1994), 150–152.

8. Susan S. Tamke, *Make a Joyful Noise* (Columbus, OH: Ohio University Press, 1978), 85.

9. Raymond F. Glover, ed., *The Hymnal 1982 Companion, Vol. Three A*, 200.

10. Tamke, 84.

11. Glover, *The Hymnal 1982 Companion, Vol. Three A*, 187.

12. F. Bland Tucker, "Reflections of a Hymn Writer," *The Hymn*, vol. 30, no. 2, April, 1979, pp. 115–116.

13. John Julian, *A Dictionary of Hymnology* (New York: Dover Publications, Inc., 1957), 1293.

14. *The Hymnal 1940 Companion* (New York: The Church Pension Fund, 1949), 40.

15. Ibid., p. 41.

16. *Imaging the Word: An Arts and Lectionary Resource* (Cleveland, OH: United Church Press, 1996)

17. Ibid., Vol. 1, 115.

18. Ibid., Vol. 1, 133.

19. Ibid., Vol. 3, 117.

20. Ibid., Vol. 3, 118.

21. Program for *A Festival of Hymns and Carols* presented by Jaroslav J. Vajda, on Sunday, Feb. 26, 1995, at the Lutheran Church of St. Philip, 2500 West Bryn Mawr, Chicago, IL.

22. Jaroslav J. Vajda, *Now the Joyful Celebration* (St. Louis: Morningstar Music Publishers, 1987), 2.

23. Ibid., 2.

24. Ibid., 10.

25. Marilyn Kay Stulken, *Hymnal Companion to the Lutheran Book of Worship* (Philadelphia: Fortress Press, 1981), 286–287.

26. Arthur Green and Barry W. Holtz, ed., *Your Word is Fire: The Hasidic Masters of Contemplative Prayer* (New York: Paulist Press, 1977), 6.

27. Percy Dearmer, *Songs of Praise Discussed* (London: Oxford University Press, 1933), 264.

28. Ibid.

29. Julian, 803.

30. Glover, ed. *The Hymnal 1982 Companion, Vol. Two*, 546.

31. Glover, ed. *The Hymnal 1982 Companion, Vol. Three B*, 1236.

32. Dietrich Bonhoeffer, *The Cost of Discipleship* (London: SCM Press Ltd., 1959), 35–36.

33. Brian Wren, *Faith Looking Forward* (Carol Stream, IL: Hope Publishing Co., 1983), "Notes," 25.

34. Thomas P. Holland and William L. Sachs, co-directors, *The Zacchaeus Project: Discerning Episcopal Identity at the Dawn of a New Millennium* (New York: The Episcopal Church Foundation, 1999), 16.

35. Glover, *The Hymnal 1982 Companion, Vol. Three B*, 1101.

36. *Hymns for Worship* (New York: Association Press, 1939), Hymn 113.

37. C.S. Lewis, *Letters to Malcolm* (New York: Harcourt, Brace & World, 1964), 75.

38. Glover, ed. *The Hymnal 1982 Companion, Vol. Two*, 393.

39. Glover, ed., *The Hymnal 1982 Companion, Vol. Three A*, 301.

40. Julian, 1149.

41. Thomas Cahill, *The Gifts of the Jews: How a Tribe of Desert Nomads Changed the Way Everyone Thinks and Feels* (New York: Nan A. Talese/Anchor Books, 1998).

42. Ibid., 63.

43. Ibid., 89.

44. Glover, ed., *The Hymnal 1982 Companion, Vol. Three B*, 693.

45. J. Dahle, *Library of Christian Hymns* (Minneapolis, 1975), 642, quoted in Glover, *The Hymnal 1982 Companion, Vol. Three B*, 1297.

46. Glover, ed. *The Hymnal 1982 Companion, Vol. Three A*, 344.

47. Julian, 426.

48. The Book of Common Prayer, 270.

49. Ronander and Porter, 180.

50. Lionel Adey, *Hymns and the Christian Myth* (Vancouver: University of British Columbia Press, 1986), 72.

51. Johann Sebastian Bach, *Kantate Nr. 140* (Leipzig: Breitkopf & Härtel, 1935), 23, 39–46.

52. Albert Edward Bailey, *The Gospel in Hymns* (New York: Charles Scribner's Sons, 1950), 353.

53. Ibid.

54. Lionel Adey, *Hymns and the Christian Myth* (Vancouver: University of British Columbia Press, 1986), 172.

55. Ronander and Porter, ed., *Guide to the Pilgrim Hymnal* (Philadelphia: United Church Press, 1966), 234.

56. The Book of Common Prayer, 334.

57. Letter to Alec Wyton from F. Bland Tucker, February 2, 1977, Church Hymnal Corporation Papers, New York, NY.

58. Theron Brown and Hezekiah Butterworth, *The Story of the Hymns and Tunes* (New York: George H. Doran Company, 1906), 98.

59. Erik Routley, *An English-Speaking Hymnal Guide* (Collegeville, MN: The Liturgical Press, 1979), 42.

60. Adey, 169–170.

61. *The Compact Edition of the Oxford English Dictionary, Vol. I* (Oxford: Oxford University Press, 1971), 1159.

62. Glover, ed., *The Hymnal 1982 Companion, Vol. Three A*, 417.

63. Stulken, 234.

64. Glover, ed., *The Hymnal 1982 Companion, Vol. Two*, 325.

65. Glover, ed., *The Hymnal 1982 Companion, Vol. Three B*, 1185.

66. Julian, 12.

67. Daw to Glover, October 15, 1986, Church Hymnal Corporation Papers, New York, NY.

68. Donald Nicholl, *Holiness* (New York: The Seabury Press, 1981), 25.

69. Ibid.

70. Ibid., 27.

71. Ibid., 25.

72. Stephen Sondheim, *Sunday in the Park with George*, Vocal Selections (New York: Revelation Music Publishing Corp., 1984), 2.

73. Percy Dearmer, *Songs of Praise Discussed* (London: Oxford University Press, 1933), 115.

74. Ibid.

75. Glover, ed. *The Hymnal 1982 Companion, Vol. Three A*, 362.

76. Erik Routley, *Hymns and the Faith* (Greenwich, CT: The Seabury Press, 1956), 71–72.

77. Ibid., 77–78.

78. Glover, ed., *The Hymnal 1982 Companion, Vol. Three B, 1150.*

79. Erik Routley, *An English-Speaking Hymnal Guide* (Collegeville, MN: The Liturgical Press, 1979), no. 410.

80. Julian, 877.

81. *The Hymnal 1940* (New York: The Church Pension Fund, 1940), Hymn 449.

82. Adey, 169.

83. Ibid., 169.

84. Glover, ed., *The Hymnal 1982 Companion, Vol. Three A*, 22.

85. Glover, ed., *The Hymnal 1982 Companion, Vol. Two*, 493.

86. *Lesser Feasts and Fasts*, Third Edition (New York: The Church Hymnal Corporation, 1980), 184.

87. F.L.Cross, *The Oxford Dictionary of the Christian Church* (Oxford: Oxford University Press, 1974), 775.

88. Albert Edward Bailey, *The Gospel in Hymns* (New York: Charles Scribner's Sons, 1950), 38.

89. Ibid.

90. Ibid., 40.

91. John Bunyan, *The Pilgrim's Progress* (New York: The Century Co., 1898), 1.

92. *The Pilgrim's Progress*, 1684 edition

93. Percy Dearmer, *Songs of Praise Discussed* (London: Oxford University Press, 1933), 271.

94. John Bunyan, *The Pilgrim's Progress From This World to That Which is to Come* (New York: The Century Co., 1898), vii.

95. John Dominic Crossan, *In Parables: The Challenge of the Historical Jesus* (New York: Harper & Row, 1973), xviii.

96. Louisa M. Alcott, *Little Women* (New York: Grosset & Dunlap, 1915), "Preface."

97. Bailey, 469.

98. Donna Meadows, "The Global Citizen," *The Valley News*, Plainfield, New Hampshire, Saturday, April 17, 1999.

99. Glover, ed., *The Hymnal 1982 Companion, Vol. Three B*, 975.

100. Ibid., 915.

101. Ibid.

102. Ibid., 916.

103. George Herbert, "The Windows," *The Country Parson, The Temple* (London: SPCK, 1981), 183.

104. Ibid., 40.

105. Bailey, 156.

106. Ibid.

107. Julian, 764–765.

108. Sofia Cavalletti, *The Religious Potential of the Child* (New York: Paulist Press, 1983).

109. Ibid., 44–45.

110. Karl Barth, *Wolfgang Amadeus Mozart* (Grand Rapids, MI: William B. Eerdmans Publishing Company, 1986), 16.

111. Ibid., 22.

112. C. S. Lewis, *The Magician's Nephew* (New York: Collier Books, 1970), 98–101.

113. Dante Alighieri, *The Divine Comedy: Volume III, Paradiso*, translated by John D. Sinclair (New York: Oxford University Press,, 1979), 109–111.

114. Ibid., 485.

115. Ibid.

116. Glover, ed., *The Hymnal Companion, Vol. Three B*, 1274.

117. Ibid., 1276.

118. *Martin Luthers Werke: Kirtische Gesamtausgabe* (Weimar, 1883–), Vol. 38, 35. Translation by Robin A. Leaver in Glover, ed., *The Hymnal 1982 Companion, Vol. Three B*, 1277.

119. Glover, ed., *The Hymnal 1982 Companion, Vol. Three B*, 1278.

120. T. G. Tappert, ed., *The Book of Concord: The Confessions of the Evangelical Lutheran Church*, (Philadelphia: Muhlenberg Press, 1959), 426–27.

121. Albert Edward Bailey, *The Gospel in Hymns* (New York: Charles Scribner's Sons, 1950), 123–124.

122. Ibid.

123. Ibid., 554.

124. Glover, ed., *The Hymnal 1982 Companion, Vol. Three B*, 1291.

125. Ibid.

126. Nancy L. Roth, *The Breath of God* (Cambridge, Massachusetts: Cowley Publications, 1990), 28.

127. Ibid., 35.

128. Nancy L. Roth, *Praying, A Book for Children* (New York: The Church Hymnal Corporation, 1991), 31.

129. Pocknee to Wallace, October 9, 1978. Church Hymnal Corporation Papers, New York, NY.

130. Timothy Ware, *The Orthodox Church* (Baltimore, MD: Penguin Books, 1964), 281.

131. Ibid., 283.

132. Frederick Buechner, *Wishful Thinking: A Seeker's ABC* (New York: Harper & Row, 1973), 95.

133. Margaret Drabble, ed., *The Oxford Companion to English Literature* (Oxford: Oxford University Press, 1985), 7.

134. Glover, ed., *The Hymnal 1982 Companion, Vol. Two*, 312.

135. Glover, ed., *The Hymnal 1982 Companion, Vol. Three B*, 781–782.

136. Ibid., 1166.

137. Ibid.

138. *The Mystical Doctrine of St. John of the Cross*, "The Ascent of Mount Carmel" (London: Sheed and Ward, 1934), 71.

139. Ibid., 83.

140. A. Haeussler, *The Story of Our Hymns* (St. Louis: Eden Publishing House, 1951), 324–325.

141. Glover, ed., *The Hymnal 1982 Companion, Vol. Three B*, 561.

142. A. G. Dickens, *The English Reformation* (New York: Schocken Books, 1964), 130.

143. Ibid., 131.

144. F. L. Cross, ed., *The Oxford Dictionary of the Christian Church* (Oxford: Oxford University Press, 1974), 1243.

145. Carlo Carretto, *Summoned by Love* (Maryknoll, NY: Orbis Books, 1978), 18–19.

146. Ibid., 19.

147. Glover, ed., *The Hymnal 1982 Companion, Vol. Three B*, 985–986.

148. The Book of Common Prayer (New York: The Church Hymnal Corp., 1979), 96.

149. Dag Hammarskjöld, *Markings* (New York: Alfred A. Knopf, 1964), 84.

150. Ninian Smart, *The Long Search* (Boston: Little, Brown and Company, 1977), 231.

151. Glover, ed., *The Hymnal 1982 Companion, Vol. Three B*, 1105.

152. *Hymnal Supplement II* (New York: Church Hymnal Corporation, 1975).

153. Albert Edward Bailey, *The Gospel in Hymns* (New York: Charles Scribner's Sons, 1950), 283.

154. Roberts and Donaldson, *The Ante-Nicene Fathers, Vol. II: Fathers of the Second Century*. (New York: Scribner's) Quoted in Albert Edward Bailey, *The Gospel in Hymns* (New York: Charles Scribner's Sons, 1950), 283–284.

155. LindaJo H. McKim, *The Presbyterian Hymnal Companion* (Louisville, KY: Westminster/John Knox Press, 1993), 288.

About the Author

The Rev. Nancy Roth has led numerous workshops and retreats in the United States and England on the subject of prayer. A native of New York, she taught music and dance before entering the General Theological Seminary in the late 1970s, where she was affiliated with the Center for Christian Spirituality. In 1981 she was ordained to the priesthood in the Diocese of New York. She was a consultant in Christian education at Trinity Church, Wall Street, where she taught courses on spirituality, and led a weekly meditation class at Manhattan Plaza, a residence for performing artists. From 1981 to 1983 she was program coordinator for Holy Cross Monastery in West Park, New York.

Her other books for Church Publishing include *Praying: a Book for Children* (1991), *We Sing of God: a Hymnal for Children* co-edited with her husband, Robert N. Roth (1989), *A Closer Walk: Meditating on Hymns for Year A* (1998), and *Awake, My Soul! Meditating on Hymns for Year B* (1999). She is also the author of *The Breath of God, A New Christian Yoga* and *Organic Prayer* (Cowley Publications) and *Meditations for Choir Members* (Morehouse). She has written the text for several hymns in *Chatter With the Angels: An Illustrated Songbook for Children* (G.I.A.).

She and her husband, a retired church musician, live in Oberlin, Ohio. Nancy Roth is working on this series of volumes of hymn meditations as an Affiliate Scholar of Oberlin College. She continues to draw on her background in music, dance, and theology, both in leading workshops, classes and retreats, and in her writing projects.